D0385733

GOD
SAW THEM THROUGH

SEMPER FI—*"AMERICA'S BATTALION"* IN IRAQ

GLENN THOMAS

CREATION
HOUSE
A STRANG COMPANY

GOD SAW THEM THROUGH by Glenn Alan Thomas
Published by Creation House Press
A Strang Company
600 Rinehart Road
Lake Mary, Florida 32746
www.creationhouse.com

This book or parts thereof may not be reproduced in any form, stored in a retrieval system, or transmitted in any form by any means—electronic, mechanical, photocopy, recording, or otherwise—without prior written permission of the publisher, except as provided by United States of America copyright law.

Unless otherwise noted, all Scripture quotations are from the New King James Version of the Bible. Copyright © 1979, 1980, 1982 by Thomas Nelson, Inc., publishers. Used by permission.

Cover design by Terry Clifton

Copyright © 2004 by Glenn Alan Thomas
All rights reserved

Library of Congress Control Number: 2004114755
International Standard Book Number: 1-59185-722-8

04 05 06 07 08— 987654321
Printed in the United States of America

DEDICATION

To Him who is able to do exceedingly abundantly beyond all that we can ask or think, and to the Marines of 2/8, together the true authors of this book.

Cpl. Jose Abarca
Lcpl. Michael Abbott
Lcpl. Tarek Abdell
Lcpl. Francisco
  Adames
Lcpl. Travis Adeboi
Cpl. Nuradin
  Afmeged
Lcpl. Lewis Aguilar
Lcpl. Justin Albanese
S. Sgt. George Albero
Pfc. Mark Albert
Pfc. Mark Aleman
Maj. Julian Alford
Lcpl. Steven Alkema
S. Sgt. Charles Allen
CWO2 Gary Allen
Cpl. Rickey Allen
S. Sgt. Steven Alverson
Cpl. Willie Anderson
S. Sgt. Kevin Andrade
Sgt. Kevin Andrade
Cpl. Timothy Apel II

HN Scott Appleby
Lcpl. Alejandro
  Arauzarios
Sgt. Gabriel Arreche
Cpl. Roberto Asanza
Pfc. Richard Ashton
Cpl. Ronald Augustine
Lcpl. Jonathan Austin
Cpl. Luis Aviles
S. Sgt. Richard Ayala
Cpl. Micah Bagby
Sgt. John Bailey II
Lcpl. Michael Baity
Lcpl. Adam Bakos
Lcpl. Mathew Baldini
Pv. Brian Banes
Lcpl. John Bard
Lcpl. Virgil Barnard
Cpl. Franklin Barnes Jr.
Lcpl. Jason Baron
Cpl. Robert Barrett
Pfc. Brian Barry
S. Sgt. William Bartels

Lcpl. Jose Basulto
Lcpl. Jermaine Bates
Sgt. Phillip Baugh
Lcpl. Jonathan
  Beaudreau
S. Sgt. Kenneth
  Becker
Pfc. Kwadwo Bediako
Lcpl. Cliffton Behner
F. Sgt. Robert Beith
Lcpl. Benjamin Bell
1st Lt. Russell Belt II
Cpl. Jesse Benavidez
2nd Lt. Charles
  Benbow
Lcpl. Brandon Benner
Lcpl. Eric Benson
Lcpl. Matthew Benson
Capt. Jeffrey Bentz
Lcpl. Halsey Bernard
Pfc. Christopher
  Bertone
Lcpl. John Best

Lcpl. Samuel Betancourt
Lcpl. Chris Betts
Cpl. Pablo Bicca
Lcpl. Russell Bishop
Cpl. Paul Biyok
Cpl. Nicholus Blackmon
Lcpl. Rodney Blackshear
Cpl. David Blair
Lcpl. Matthew Blair
Lcpl. Nathaniel Blanton
2nd Lt. Mathias Boehn
Lcpl. David Bohner
Cpl. David Boland
Lcpl. Jason Bolton
Lcpl. Christopher Borowiec
S. Sgt. Raymond Botsford
2nd Lt. Zaner Bouza
Lcpl. Nathan Braden
Cpl. Benjamin Bradford
Lcpl. Joshua Bradway
Cpl. Jason Branch
Lcpl. Adam Bras
Cpl. Joseph Brockbank
M. Gy. Sgt. Charles Broda
Lcpl. Maxwell Brom
Lcpl. Bryan Brooker
Lcpl. Wayne Brown
Lcpl. Esquire Brown

Lcpl. Christopher Browning
G. Sgt. Barrington Bruce
Lcpl. Thomas Bruns
Lcpl. James Brunson
Cpl. Jason Bryant
Lcpl. Christopher Buchanan
Lcpl. Nathaniel Buchholtz
Pfc. Cory Buffalo
Pfc. James Burch
Cpl. James Burke
Pfc. Benjamin Burnett
Cpl. Wesley Burnett
Sgt. Chad Burns
Pfc. David Burton
Lcpl. Justin Burza
Lcpl. Christopher Bush
Cpl. Robert Butler
Lcpl. Joseph Cacciapaglia
Lcpl. John Cain Jr.
HN James Calhoun
Sgt. Kenneth Campbell
Lcpl. Randy Campbell
WO Christopher Campbell
Lcpl. Kevin Cannon
Pv. Darren Cansler
Lcpl. James Capretti
Lcpl. Alfred Carr
G. Sgt. Paul Carr
G. Sgt. Stephen Carr
Lcpl. Adrian Carrillo
Sgt. Joseph Carter IV

Lcpl. Dustin Cathcart
Cpl. Roberto Cazares
Cpl. Anthony Ceccacci
Lcpl. Carlos Centeno
Lcpl. Juan Cervantes
Lcpl. Michael Chadwick II
S. Sgt. Wayne Chambers
Lcpl. Richard Chandler
Lcpl. Ryan Chapman
Cpl. Charles Charlson
Cpl. Matthew Charron
Lcpl. Timothy Chow
Cpl. Anthony Ciesielski
Pfc. Jeff Clapp
Lcpl. Ryan Clay
Cpl. Wyatt Clevenger
Cpl. Timothy Clossin
Lcpl. James Cobb Jr.
Cpl. Stephen Coffee
Lcpl. John Colby Jr.
Lcpl. Tony Coleman
Cpl. John Coleman III
Cpl. Victor Colindres
Lcpl. Justin Collins
Cpl. Joel Connick
HN Chad Contranchis
HM3 Cristian Contreras
Lcpl. Fabian Contrerassalas
Lcpl. Brian Cook
Lcpl. Matthew Copeland
Lcpl. Paul Corbett II
HM3 Carlos Cordovarosa

Dedicated to...

Cpl. Richard Corea
Cpl. Juan Cortez
Pv. Mike Cortez
Lcpl. Roderik Cosio
Lcpl. Joe Costilla
Lcpl. Michael Coston
Lcpl. Alexander Covell
Sgt. Shane Cowen
Pfc. Herman Cox
1st Lt. Eric Craig
Sgt. Bryan Cridell
Lcpl. Jesse Crofton
Lcpl. Donald Crutcher
Pfc. Edward Cruz
Lcpl. Ryan Cullen
Lcpl. Jason Cummings
Pfc. Timothy Curry
G. Sgt. William Cutrer
Lcpl. Harold Daines
Cpl. Douglas Danielson
Lcpl. David Danukos
Pfc. Clinton Darquea
Cpl. Jesse Davis
Lcpl. Joseph Davis
Cpl. Patrick Davis
Lcpl. Terry Davis
Lcpl. Wayland Davis
Lcpl. Richard Deal
Lcpl. Quintin Degroot
Cpl. Guillermo Delaparra
Cpl. Luis Deleon
HM2 Alan Dementer
2nd Lt. Christopher Demetriades
S. Sgt. Robert Dennis
Lcpl. David Densmore

Cpl. Keith Denton
Pv. Kenneth Deppen
Lcpl. Mathew Desimone
Pfc. Jarrod Despres
Cpl. Jared Detton
Lcpl. David Diazconcepcion
Lcpl. Federico Diazmartinez
Cpl. John Dicesare
Lcpl. Eric Dietrich
Lcpl. Curtis Diggs
Lcpl. James Dinella
S. Sgt. Wesley Dinsmore
Lcpl. Orlando Dominguez Jr.
Cpl. Jon Donald
Lcpl. Joshua Donald
Cpl. Shawn Dooling
Lcpl. Stephen Doublet
Lcpl. Dominic Dougherty
Pfc. Michael Douglas
Capt. Timothy Dremann Jr.
Lcpl. Thomas Drury
Pfc. Geoffrey Duenez
Lcpl. Mark Duncan
Lcpl. Randy Dunkel
Capt. John Dupree
Lcpl. Adam Dyer
Lcpl. Donniejack Earhart
Lcpl. Joseph Earle
Lcpl. Robert Eastman
Cpl. Nicholas Eddington

Cpl. Jonathan Eldridge
S. Sgt. Kevin Ellicott
Pfc. James Ellis
Lcpl. Justin Ellis
Lcpl. Aaron Elrod
Lcpl. Daniel Engle
Pfc. Jared Ernest
S. Sgt. James Erwin Jr.
Sgt. Jean Espino
HM3 Alexander Espinoza
Lcpl. Jonathan Faff
Cpl. Gabriel Fajardo
HN Douglas Farmer
Cpl. Nicholas Farmer
Cpl. Maurice Fenner
Sgt. Edward Ferguson
Lcpl. Lydell Ferguson
Sgt. Stanley Ferguson
Lcpl. Jaime Fernandez
Lcpl. Gavin Fields
HN Wade Finch
Lcpl. Daniel Fincher
Cpl. Brian Findley
2nd Lt. Matthew Fitzsimmons
Lcpl. John Flaminia
Lcpl. William Flick
Lcpl. Erik Flores
HN Oscarfloyd Flores
Pfc. David Floyd
2nd Lt. George Flynn
Lcpl. Brandon Fojtasek
WO Jason Forgash
Cpl. Cliff Foster
Lcpl. Kristian Foster
Lcpl. William Foster Jr.

Dedicated to...

Cpl. Charles Francis
Cpl. Robert Franko III
Cpl. John Friend
Lcpl. Christopher Frost
Lcpl. Terren Frye
Lcpl. Javier Fuentes
Maj. Robert Fulford
Lcpl. Matthew Fuller
Lcpl. Nicholas Fulmer
Lcpl. David Gallegos
Cpl. Michael Gallineaux
Lcpl. Nathan Gamboa
Lcpl. Matthew Gammon
Sgt. Troy Gandolfi
Lcpl. Jessie Garcia
Lcpl. Jaime Garcialira
Cpl. Martin Garcia-Lopez
F. Sgt. Howard Gatewood
Lcpl. Jesse Gaydos
Cpl. Patrick Gaynor
S. Sgt. Richard Gibbs
1st Lt. Benjamin Gifford
Sgt. James Glegola
Sgt. Darin Gloede
S. Sgt. Timothy Glore
Cpl. Caleb Goforth
Lcpl. Brian Gonzales
Lcpl. Diego Gonzales
Cpl. William Gonzales III
Cpl. Miguel Gonzalez
Lcpl. Jonah Gonzalez

2nd Lt. Daniel Goodkofsky
Cpl. Andrew Goodrich
Cpl. Tavia Goss
Lcpl. Brandon Gowdy
Lcpl. Richard Graff Jr.
Lcpl. James Grandmaison
Lcpl. Todd Grant
Pfc. Patrick Gravenese Jr.
Cpl. Brenan Gray
Lcpl. Jonathan Green
S. Sgt. Anthony Greene
Cpl. Damian Gregoire
Lcpl. Shaun Gridley
Lcpl. Cary Griffin
Lcpl. David Griffith
Pfc. Ross Groscup
Lcpl. Joseph Gross
Lcpl. Benjamin Grover Jr.
Pfc. David Grubb
Lcpl. Thomas Gudmundsson
Lcpl. Carlos Guerra
Cpl. Jory Guidry
Lcpl. Jeffery Gunn II
Cpl. Kevan Guyton
Lcpl. Brian Hafner
Lcpl. Shawn Hale
G. Sgt. Tracy Hale
G. Sgt. Aubery Hall
Cpl. Wallace Hall
Sgt. Michael Halterman

Cpl. Steven Hammond
Lcpl. John Hancock
Lcpl. William Hancock
G. Sgt. Timothy Haney
Lcpl. Justin Hardy
HN Bryan Harris
CWO2 Christopher Harris
Lcpl. Jonathan Harris
Cpl. Roddney Harris
Capt. Theodore Haskell
Lcpl. Phillip Hastings
1st Lt. Carl Havens
G. Sgt. John Hawkins
Pfc. Ty Hawkinson
Cpl. James Hay
Sgt. Douglas Hayden
Cpl. Joshua Hayden
Lcpl. Thomas Hays
Lcpl. Eric Hazelwood
Lcpl. Jonathan Healzer
Lcpl. Charles Hecksher
2nd Lt. William Hefty
Lcpl. Joshua Henderson
Sgt. Bruce Henning
Lcpl. Christopher Henry
G. Sgt. Willard Henry
Lcpl. Julio Hernandez
Lcpl. Oscar Hernandez
Cpl. Jesse Herrera
Lcpl. Alvin Hickman
Lcpl. Paul Hicks
S. Sgt. Donald Higgins
Lcpl. Kymball Hight

Dedicated to...

Lcpl. Corey Hill
S. Sgt. Karem Hill
Lcpl. Tavare Hill
Sgt. Warren Hills
Cpl. Jesse Hines
Cpl. Chad Hiser
Lcpl. Joshua Hoag
Maj. John Hogan
HM1 Michael Holmes
Lcpl. Mishawn Holt
Lcpl. Jessie Holton
Sgt. Steven Holtrop
Cpl. Ben Holy
Lcpl. Allan Hone
Lcpl. Jonathan Hoover
Lcpl. Jeffrey Hopson
Cpl. Sidney Horton
Lcpl. Jason Houser
G. Sgt. Chester Howe
Lcpl. Scott Hoy
Lcpl. Timothy Huff
1st Lt. Patrick Hulsy
Lcpl. Brandon Humm
HN John Huncher
Cpl. Noah Hunsaker
Lcpl. James Hutchison
Cpl. Maurice Hyson Jr.
HN Daniel Immediato
Pfc. Justin Itri
Lcpl. David Jackson
Lcpl. Eric Jaekle
Lcpl. John Jankowski
Lcpl. Damian Jenkins
Lcpl. Charley Jennings
Cpl. Erik Jennings
Cpl. Juan Jimenez
Cpl. Richard Jimenez
Cpl. Robert Johncox
HMC David Johnsen

Cpl. Brian Johnson
Lcpl. David Johnson
Lcpl. Justin Johnson
Sgt. Eric Johnson
Cpl. Charles Jones
Cpl. Jesse Jones
2nd Lt. John Jones
Lcpl. Loren Jones
Cpl. Timothy Jones
Cpl. Eric Jorgensen
Lcpl. Bobby Joseph
Sgt. Raiff Josey
Lcpl. Cesar Juarez
Pfc. Joshua Juristy
Pfc. Jack Kandel
Lcpl. Izeth Kane
Lcpl. Justin Keiser
Capt. John Keller
Lcpl. Jeremy Kenison
Pfc. Shane Kent
Pfc. Mark Kes
Cpl. Adam Kestner
Lcpl. Michael Kiley
Lcpl. Dominic Kimzey
Lcpl. Michael Kinard
Lcpl. Kevin King
Lcpl. Timothy Kinnard
Lcpl. Jason Kinsella
Lcpl. Larry Kirkland
Lcpl. Brain Klarich
Lcpl. Caleb Kleinpeter
Lcpl. Robert Knapp
Lcpl. Christopher
  Knight
Lcpl. Noah Knight
Lcpl. Jerome
  Knochelman II
Sgt. Josef Kocsis
Cpl. David Kophamer

Cpl. Keith Kosirog
Sgt. Michael Kotter
Cpl. Seth Kozlowski
Lcpl. Jason Kreig
Pv. Matthew Kujda
Lcpl. Chaichana
  Kulvanish
Cpl. Daniel Lain
Sgt. Edwardo
  Lamboy Jr.
Pfc. Jeffrey Landreth
Lcpl. Dustin Lanehart
Cpl. Sean Laney
Cpl. Charles Langley
Pfc. Matthew
  Langworthy
Lcpl. Shawn Lantry
Lcpl. Ryan Larson
Lcpl. Richard Laux
Lcpl. William Lawhon
Cpl. David Leclair
Lcpl. Andrew Lee
HN Tomichi Lee
Cpl. Corey Lee
Cpl. Lucien Lege
Pfc. Jeff Lehman
Lcpl. Benjamin
  Leibolt
Cpl. John Leon Jr.
Cpl. Juan Lerma
2nd Lt. Thomas Leslie
HM2 Dexter Lewis
Pfc. Mark Lickliter
Lcpl. Ryan Light
Lcpl. Derrick Lilly
Lcpl. Rosendo
  Limon Jr.
Cpl. Steven Link
Lcpl. Joseph Lipps

Dedicated to...

Lcpl. James Longoria
Lcpl. Christian Lopez
Lcpl. Juan Lopez
Cpl. Alfredo Lopez
Sgt. Michael Loud
Lcpl. Johnie Lovitt
Cpl. Terrell Lowe
Lcpl. Sean Luce
Capt. Benjamin
   Luciano
Lcpl. Matthew Lugo
2nd Lt. Carlos Luna
Lcpl. Trent Lundeen
Lcpl. John Lutcher
Lcpl. Jamie Lynch
Lcpl. Willis Lynn II
Capt. Seth
   Maccutcheon
Lcpl. Andrew Mack
Cpl. Michael Mackay
HN Mark Madole
Cpl. Francisco
   Madrigal
Lcpl. Thomas
   Madziarek
Cpl. Sean Mahoney
Cpl. Patrick Main
Cpl. Michael Malone
Lcpl. Jeremy
   Manchester
Lcpl. Alexander
   Manin
Pfc. Joshua
   Margwarth
HM3 Travis Markel
Lcpl. Travis Marsik
Lcpl. David Martell
Cpl. Blaine Martin
Sgt. Donald Martin Jr.

Lcpl. Andres Martinez
Lcpl. Antonio
   Martinez
HM2 Ronnie
   Mashburn
Cpl. Erik Mason
Lcpl. Omar Mata
Cpl. Christopher
   Mccain
Sgt. James Mccauley
Lcpl. Joseph
   McCelland
Lcpl. Michael
   McCormick
Lcpl. William
   McCormick
Lcpl. Aaron McCoy
Lcpl. Jacob McDonald
Lcpl. David
   McFadden
Cpl. Alexander
   McIntyre
Cpl. Kelvin McMillan
Cpl. Raymond
   McMurray
Sgt. Travis McNerney
HM2 Victor Mechanye
1st Lt. Ricardo Medal
Cpl. Jeffrey Meier
Cpl. Gustavo Mejia
Sgt. Alfonso Mejia Jr.
Lcpl. Joshua Menard
Lcpl. Elvis Mendoza
Pfc. J. Meng
Pv. Matthew Mengel
Lcpl. Winter Mercedes
HM3 Jeff Merkel
Lcpl. Anthony
   Michaels

Cpl. Craig Miller
Lcpl. Chad Milquet
Lcpl. Corey Minton
Cpl. Anthony Miozza
Lcpl. Michael
   Mohawk
Lcpl. Troy Mohrland
Cpl. Wilmer
   Mojicamartinez
Lcpl. Ai Moksivong
Sgt. Wellington
   Molina
HM3 Jose Monreal Jr.
Cpl. Jerome Moody Jr.
Cpl. Johnny Moore
M. Sgt. Reginald
   Moore
Capt. John Moore
Cpl. Daniel Mora
Pfc. Jose Morales Jr.
S. Sgt. Brett Moree
HM1 David Morin
Lcpl. Duane Morris
Lcpl. Justin Morris
Pfc. Kevin Morrison
Pv. Eric Morrone
Cpl. Ronald Morrow
Capt. Travis Morse
Lt. Col. Royal
   Mortenson
Lcpl. Eric Moss
Cpl. Jason Muldovan
Pfc. Alvin Muller
Sgt. Clinton Mullins
Cpl. Diego Muniz
Lcpl. Elias Munoz
Cpl. Angel Munoz II
Sgt. Christopher
   Murphy

Dedicated to...

1st Lt. Jamie Murphy
Lcpl. Richard Murphy
Lcpl. David Murray
Cpl. Wayne Mydlinski Jr.
Pfc. Kevin Nash
Lcpl. Chimdi Naze
Lcpl. Efrain Negron
Cpl. Derrick Nelson
Cpl. Quincy Newman
Lcpl. Jordan Newton
1st Lt. Matthew Nicholas
Lcpl. Chavis Nicholls
Cpl. Kyle Nichols
Cpl. Damon Niese
Lcpl. James Nobiletti
1st Lt. Gregory Nolan
Cpl. Vladimyr Norgaisse
Lcpl. Miguel Noriega
Lcpl. Milan Obradovic
Sgt. Brian Ocallahan
Lcpl. Jacob O'Dell
1st Lt. Dennis O'Donnell
Pfc. David Offutt Jr.
Lcpl. Paul Oliver
Lcpl. Elijah Olsen
Lcpl. Charles Olson
Cpl. Victoriano Ornelas
Lcpl. Andre Ortiz
Lcpl. Danny Ortiz
Pfc. Jose Ortiz
2nd Lt. Nathan Osbrach
Lcpl. Kevin Ott
Pfc. Timothy Otto

Lcpl. Willie Outlaw
HN Nicholas Owens
1st Lt. Tomomi Owens
Lcpl. Derrick Pace
S. Sgt. Gerardo Padilla
Pfc. Steven Pagano
Lcpl. Eldion Pajollari
Cpl. Jesus Paltasinchi
Cpl. Jose Pargas
Lcpl. Hye Keun Park
Lcpl. John Parker
Cpl. Timothy Parker
S. Sgt. Clinton Parks
G. Sgt. Anthony Pastella
Lcpl. Kunal Patel
S. Sgt. George Patten
Pfc. Aubrey Paul
HM1 Richard Paul
Lcpl. Kenneth Pauli
Cpl. Derek Payton
Cpl. Ted Pazik
Lcpl. John Peacock Jr.
Cpl. Daryl Pearl
Lcpl. Brandon Peavy
Pfc. John Pendlebury Jr.
Cpl. Armando Perez
Sgt. Roberto Perez
HM3 Rey Perez
Cpl. Levi Perkins
Cpl. Timothy Perkins
Cpl. Clifford Perry
Pfc. Anthony Persiani
Lcpl. Dareld Peterson
Sgt. Paul Phillips
Lcpl. Dennis Pichardo
Pfc. Joseph Pienta
Pfc. David Pierce

Cpl. Diordane Pierrelouis
Lcpl. George Pierson
Pfc. Hakeen Pinkston
Cpl. Christophe Pitlocksalas
Lcpl. Luke Poljak
Lcpl. Reginald Porter
Sgt. Sean Powers
S. Sgt. Robert Pratt
Lcpl. Jamie Praylow
Cpl. Thomas Preston
Lcpl. Brooks Price
Lcpl. Micah Price
Pfc. Juan Prieto
Pfc. Steven Pritchett
Lcpl. Evan Proctor
Lcpl. Luis Quinones
Cpl. Anibal Quinones-Rosado
1st Lt. Chad Ragan
Lcpl. David Ramirez
Cpl. Pete Ramirez Jr.
HN Nelson Ramos
Cpl. Nemecio Ramos
Lcpl. Nilton Ramos
Lcpl. Ramon Ramos
Pfc. Juan Ramoschavez
Pfc. Joseph Randolphi
HN James Reed
Lcpl. Christopher Renehan
Lcpl. Lavoid Rentas
Sgt. Camilo Reyes
Cpl. Daniel Rheaume
Lcpl. Christopher Richards

Dedicated to...

Lcpl. Dontrelle Richards
S. Sgt. Ewan Richards
Lcpl. Rufus Riddick III
HN Brylan Riggins
Cpl. Kim Riley Jr.
Cpl. Alex Rivera
Cpl. Harold Rivera
Lcpl. Devlin Robinson
Cpl. Jerry Robinson
Lcpl. James Robles
Cpl. Anthony Robson
Cpl. Carlos Rocha
Lcpl. Carlos Rodriguez
Lcpl. Damien Rodriguez
Lcpl. Esteban Rodriguez
Lcpl. Fidel Rodriguez
Cpl. Jiovanie Rodriguez
Cpl. Johnny Rodriguez
Pfc. Jose Rodriguez
Lcpl. Joshua Rodriguez
Cpl. Ricky Rodriguez
Lcpl. Luis Rodriguez Jr.
Lcpl. Erwin Rodrillo
Sgt. Todd Rogers
Lt. Donald Rogers Jr.
Lcpl. Ramon Rojas Jr.
Lcpl. Julio Roman
Cpl. Douglas Romine
Lcpl. Robert Romines
Lcpl. Mike Rose
Capt. Brian Ross
Lcpl. Eric Ross
Lcpl. Hylan Rousseau
S. Sgt. Jeremy Rowland
Lcpl. Daniel Rowles

Lcpl. Brad Ruetschi
Lcpl. Alfred Ruggles
2nd Lt. Blair Ruhling
S. Sgt. Alex Russell
Capt. James Ryans
Lcpl. Robert Ryles
Pfc. Joseph Sackett
Pfc. John Sala
Lcpl. Miguel Salazar
HM3 Luis Salgado
Cpl. Christopher Samiadjibenthin
Lcpl. Daniel Sampson
Lcpl. Juan Sanchez
Cpl. Jeromy Sanders
HM3 Juan Sandoval
Cpl. Raymond Sandoval
Lcpl. Nigel Sands
Pfc. Kerry Sans
Lcpl. Oj Santamaria
Lcpl. Albert Santillan
Lcpl. Ernesto Santillan Jr.
Cpl. Matthew Santoro
Sgt. Daniel Schaefer
Pfc. Nicholas Schauer
Cpl. Richard Scheffler III
Sgt. Matthew Schettler
Pfc. Mathew Schindler
Lcpl. Hank Schrader
Pfc. Mathew Schulz
Pfc. Jamarr Scott
Sgt. Jared Scott
S. Sgt. Harold Scott Jr.
Lcpl. William Seay
Pfc. Kevin Seidita
Cpl. Michael Sellars

Lcpl. Gabriel Sharrock
S. Sgt. Vernon Sheldon
Lcpl. Thomas Siau
Cpl. Shawn Sierra
Lcpl. Dean Simmons
Sgt. James Simmons
Sgt. Darnell Sims
S. Sgt. James Sippial
Pfc. James Sirmons
1st Lt. Thomas Siverts
Lcpl. Jason Smedley
Lcpl. Aaron Smith
Pfc. Charronn Smith
Pfc. Donnie Smith
Lcpl. Eric Smith
Cpl. Leelan Smith
Lcpl. Todd Soucie
2nd Lt. Kris Southwick
Lcpl. Joshua Speer
Pfc. Scott Spencer
Sgt. Jimmy Spivey
G. Sgt. Robert Sprouse
F. Sgt. William Squires
Cpl. Sipha Sreiy
S. Sgt. Ricky St John
Pfc. Anthony Stahlman
Cpl. Richard Starling
HN Matthew Staszak
Lcpl. Samuel Stavroff
Lcpl. Nicholas Stavros
Lcpl. Daniel Stephens
2nd Lt. Matthew Stephens
Pfc. Timothy Sterling
Sgt. Anthony Stewart
Cpl. Jamie Stoffer
Lcpl. John Stogsdill
Lcpl. Jaworiska Story
Pfc. Martin Story II

Dedicated to…

Pfc. Joshua Stout
Cpl. Mackerl
    Stuckey Jr.
Lcpl. Matthew Sullivan
Pfc. Barry Sward
Pfc. Jason Swayzee
G. Sgt. William
    Sweeney
Cpl. Scott Swett Jr.
Cpl. Michael Tacke
Lcpl. Jimmy Tackett
Cpl. Antonio Tafoya
Lcpl. Corey Taylor
Lt. Jerome Taylor
2nd Lt. Robert Taylor
Sgt. Richard Tchicaya
Lcpl. Mark Theis
Lcpl. David Thomas
HM1 Patrick
    Thompson
F. Sgt. Myles Thorne
HN Don Tindle
Lcpl. Gilberto Torres
Lcpl. Michael Torres
Lcpl. John Tracz
Sgt. Varavut Treme
Sgt. Joshua Tretter
Cpl. Douglas Turner
Lt. Samuel Turner
Cpl. Erik Uecke
1st Lt. James Uwins
Lcpl. Jarret Vaden
Pfc. Leighton Valencia
Cpl. Andy Van Orden
Lcpl. Edward Vargas
Cpl. Chad Vasquez
HN Robert Vause
Cpl. Alejandro Veliz
Pfc. Jhems Vernet

Cpl. Joseph Vetter
Lcpl. Daniel Vickers
S. Sgt. Patrick Virgile
Sgt. Thomas Voelkel
Sgt. Ross Wafler
Lcpl. David Walker
G. Sgt. Michael Walker
Cpl. Jevonni Walton
Lcpl. Justin Walts
Pfc. Eric Ward
Pfc. Timothy Warner
Cpl. Timothy Warren
Lcpl. Kenneth
    Washington
Lcpl. James Watson
Pfc. James Weaver
S. Sgt. Homer Webb
HN James Webb
Cpl. Marcus Weisbarth
M. Sgt. Darryl Wells
Pfc. John Wettlaufer
Cpl. Sean Whalen
Lcpl. Donald
    Whetstone
Lcpl. Anthony White
Pfc. Dustin Whitehead
Pfc. William
    Whitelatch
Pfc. Travis
    Whitherspoon
Lcpl. Benjamin Whye
Cpl. Jacob Wilcken
Cpl. Richard Wilcox III
Sgt. Christoper Wilkin
Lcpl. Benjamin Willard
F. Sgt. Clark Williams
Lcpl. Frederick
    Williams
Lcpl. Robert Williams

Lcpl. Dwayne
    Williamson
Sgt. Neil Williamson
Lcpl. Nicholas
    Williamson
Cpl. James Wilson
HM3 Samuel
    Winston Jr.
Cpl. Clinton
    Wisebaker
Cpl. Joshua
    Wittenauer
Cpl. Krzysztof
    Wlazlinski
Sgt. Eric Wolf
Cpl. Lawrence Wolfe
2nd Lt. Jeffrey Wong
Lcpl. Adam Woodburn
Cpl. Bret Woolhether
Cpl. David
    Worswick Jr.
Lcpl. Benjamin Wright
S. Sgt. Lakendrick
    Wright
Cpl. Trevor Wright
Lcpl. Robert Yancer
Lcpl. John Yang
Capt. Kevin Yeo
Lcpl. Barnaby Yoder
Lcpl. Joseph York
Cpl. Shawn Young
Cpl. Marc Zacharias
Sgt. Steven Zakar
Lcpl. John Zenk
Cpl. John Zonneveld
Lcpl. William Zumbro

ACKNOWLEDGMENTS

THERE ARE MANY 2/8 MARINES, family members, friends, and associates who deserve acknowledgment and my heartfelt thanks and appreciation for their undying support and encouragement throughout the effort to write this book. It would have been an impossible task without their help and assistance to accurately and fully turn into this tangible record what started for me as an inner desire to document the story of 2/8 in Operation Iraqi Freedom. Thankfully, God had been placing the same desire on many of their hearts as well, and I can truly say that it has been a labor of love to the Lord to carry on with this work.

I can't give enough thanks and credit to several of the 2/8 Marines, their wives, and families in particular who were so willing to give of their time and efforts. Their enthusiasm and support, and especially their patience and willingness to educate me and provide an incredibly insightful look into their world as Marines and Marine families, were most helpful. These include Royal and Leann Mortenson, Rob Fulford, Brian and Tracy Ross, Rich and Catherine Dremann, Kevin and Andrea Yeo, Dale and Jennifer Alford, and Chad and Becky Ragan. I thank all 2/8 and RCT-2 Marines who consented to my requests for interviews and to provide information including many of the pictures included in this book. These include Ronald Bailey, Donald Rogers, Ben Luciano, Jim Ryans, John Robert Dupree, Howard Gatewood, Gordon Ritchie, Jeff Wong, John Friend, John Cain, Dameon Rodriguez, Miguel Noriega, Eric Ross, Brad Ruetschi, and William Squires.

The extended families of John Cain and Kevin and Andrea Yeo were also most helpful. John's mother, Ruth, and father, John, his sister Jennifer Peterson, Kevin's mother, Delores, and Andrea's sister, Patricia Williams, all provided many details and much encouragement. Elizabeth Menard and Ben Shook provided testimonies and story details that are greatly appreciated. Dr. Richard Pritchard was very forthcoming in his testimony and deserves our genuine appreciation for his continuing service to the Lord and America. I would like to especially thank Carlton Fulford for his willingness to write what is a stirring and sincere foreword. Many thanks are due Kerry Sanders of NBC-TV for his active support by providing story details, for his thoughtful and lucid introduction, and for his help in securing use in the book of the images captured by fellow embedded journalists, including Chris Bouroncle of AFP. A special note of thanks and appreciation are due Chuck Colson, who took time from his extremely busy ministry schedule to review and recommend this book.

I consider the commitment and partnership with the people of Strang Communications to be the perfect answer from God to our prayers and efforts to publish this story. Starting with the rapid response to our submission from Bert Ghezzi, the Editorial Director at the Strang Book Group, the professional and deeply committed staff at Strang Communications and Creation House Press have been a joy to work with. Lee Grady, Allen Quain,

Ginny Maxwell, Atalie Anderson, Woodley Auguste, and others have been both partners and mentors, and the strong fellowship in Christ we have experienced has been a blessing to me. May God continue to bless all that you corporately and individually put your hands to do for Him.

Several work associates of mine have been especially supportive and encouraging, including Anne Sweeney, Wendy Huttner, and Jeff Deal. A heartfelt thanks is due Jeff for proofreading the manuscript. A note of thanks also is due Anthony Ubal for his work in creating the maps and organizational charts included in the book. And a special thank you is due Chris Collins for his partnership and for his creative ideas that were incorporated throughout this effort.

My foremost appreciation and thanks go to my wife, Pam, sons David and Nathan, daughters Kelly, Rebecca, and Sarah and soon to be daughter-in-law, Erin Hawkins, whose prayers and enthusiasm have helped continually to spur me onwards. David, in essence, started the whole effort to write a book with his telephone call home from the USS Saipan back in May 2003 as he and 2/8 were beginning their return trip from the war in Iraq. It is a day I will never forget, for it was so plainly evident that God had really done something special with the battalion and with him. And I am truly thankful for the words of wisdom that God spoke through Pam, helping to direct and make the right decisions at the right time. She truly is the unsung heroine of our family, a wife and mother whose behind-the-scenes work in raising our children and whose love, care, and concern for us all is of immeasurable value.

In closing, with an admittedly certain amount of bias, Pam and I dare to say that as the generation of Americans that includes the majority of 2/8 Marines and our children continues to fight and win the physical war against terrorism and continues to fight for the Lord's kingdom on earth through prayer and selfless service, the future of America is indeed most bright.

May God's blessings be upon all involved and all who read this true-life adventure.

—GLENN ALAN THOMAS
EAST AMHERST, NEW YORK

Contents

Foreword

I lift up my eyes to the hills—where does my help come from? My help comes from the Lord, the Maker of heaven and earth. He will not let your foot slip—he who watches over you will not slumber; indeed he who watches over Israel will neither slumber nor sleep. The Lord watches over you—the Lord is your shade at your right hand; the sun will not harm you by day, nor the moon by night. The Lord will keep you from all harm—he will watch over your life; the Lord will watch over your coming and going, both now and forevermore.

—Psalm 121, NIV

I T IS AN HONOR FOR me to pen the foreword for *God Saw Them Through*. As the father of Major Rob Fulford, 2/8's Operations Officer, I have a firsthand knowledge of the events Glenn Thomas so vividly describes in the pages that follow.

By way of introduction, I am a proud Christian, husband, and father of three. I retired from the Marine Corps in February 2003, after thirty-seven years of active service. Throughout my Marine Corps career, I had the unique privilege of leading Marines through the rigors of combat in Vietnam in 1967 through 1968; and in Operation Desert Shield/Desert Storm as the Commanding Officer, Regimental Combat Team 7 (RCT-7: TF Ripper). Each of my combat experiences was unique in their terrain and the enemy.

However, the similarities were striking in the way they brought me closer to the Lord and strengthened my personal faith.

An often-heard cliché is that "there are no atheists in combat." From my personal experience, this is an accurate statement. Combat brings individuals face to face with their own mortality, forcing all of us to search out our relationships with our Creator. Additionally, the emotional strain of combat can take a significant toll on the mental psyche of those serving, especially the commanders.

Psalm 121 at the beginning of this page is very special to me because it was sent to me by my son, Rob, in the Fall of 1990. At the time, I was leading RCT-7, defending Saudi Arabia, and preparing to be the lead element on the Marine assault into Kuwait. I was feeling quite down, and those feelings had come out in a recent letter home to my son. Rob's response letter lifted my spirits by reminding me to read the Psalmist's words closely—"The Lord watches over you."

Knowing firsthand the power of God's protection in combat, I never truly appreciated the power of a praying nation until this latest conflict. Unlike my previous combat experience, I was not a participant in Operation Iraqi Freedom. For the first time in over three decades, I watched as our nation's military prepared and executed a magnificent campaign. The helpless feeling of sending a child off to war is something I was not prepared for, however. My wife and I relied solely on the Lord during this period, praying like so many other mothers and fathers for the safe return of our children.

I encourage every reader, military and civilian, to carefully consider the story contained in these pages. Simply, it is a story about family—spiritual family, physical family, and the Marine Corps family. The Lord truly watched over and protected the Marines of "America's Battalion," and I, like so many other parents, am eternally grateful for that fact.

—CARLTON W. FULFORD, JR.,
GENERAL, UNITED STATES MARINE CORPS, RETIRED

INTRODUCTION

BY KERRY SANDERS

WHEN THE STORIES ARE TOLD and the war is dissected, the indisputable facts remain: the battle in An-Nasiriyah was pivotal. Consider: the U.S. Military battle plan was hindered before it began. The U.S. Army 4th ID could not come in from the west as planned because Turkey's politicians said no.

As we would see, the march to Baghdad was from the South. And standing between U.S. forces and Saddam Hussein's capital: An-Nasiriyah, or "the Naz" as it become known.

As you read on, you'll discover a slice of history won by the brave men of the 2nd Battalion, 8th Marines.

How did I end up there to see it all?

Weeks before, I was sitting in a five star hotel in downtown

Kuwait wondering "if there is going to be a war, how will I ever cover it?"

I knew journalists who had been selected by their news organizations to enjoy the high-profile slots as embedded journalists. NBC did not choose me for that assignment.

I was told because of my reporting in previous conflicts, such as Haiti, Kosovo, and Afghanistan, that they thought I'd be a perfect choice to report as a "unilateral reporter." In this case, unilateral reporting was different and I knew that. It could be fatal. A unilateral reporter goes off on his own to see developments.

On this battlefield, being in the wrong place at the wrong time could mean being killed by the U.S. forces just as easily as it could mean getting killed by Iraqi troops.

Instead I opted to try something else. I decided to suggest to the commanding officer with the 2/8 that we create an embed. It would be off-the-books. It would not be sanctioned by the brass in the Pentagon but I figured come wartime, who would look over a list and say "Hey, they don't belong there. Yank them out"?

With that theory swimming in my head, I loaded up our NBC humvee and headed out into the Kuwaiti desert to chat up Lt. Col. Royal Mortenson. Our twelve-year old, rebuilt humvee was in sad shape, but it made it out to camp. There I pried the Lt. Col. away from pressing war-planning business to hit him up. "What would you think of blah blah blah..." He cut me off, "You're trying to cut a drug deal, aren't you?"

"A drug deal?" I said.

"A drug deal!" he said.

For those of you as unfamiliar with military-speak as I was, "a drug deal" is an off-the-books agreement that benefits everyone.

In the dust of the desert, near a water buffalo, we made "the drug deal." I was joining the 2/8 with an NBC News team. Cameraman Sebastian Rich and satellite engineer Danny Miller were on for the challenge. We made no promises of what we would report. The good, the bad, and the ugly would all go on our television reports. A confident Lt. Col. Royal Mortenson had no qualms. He had confidence in his men. He knew they would make the U.S. Marines proud. He also knew Americans would be proud to see the sacrifices made in wartime.

Our NBC News team moved into the camp, and within two weeks we were on our way to Iraq. Before we left, a young Marine asked me, "Why are you coming with us? We're not going to see any action, you know." He went on to explain that this war was for the Pendleton Marines, not the Marines from Camp Lejeune. He said at most the Marines from Lejuene would guard a highway intersection.

As you will read in the pages that follow, once in "the Naz," it was anything but quiet.

I thank the 2/8 for their honesty and their ability to fight a war with three newsmen tagging along, reporting developments live on NBC and MSNBC. This was first war reported live on the television screens around the world.

It took heaps of courage for the 2/8 to trust outsiders.

I feel after our shared experience we are no longer outsiders. We are the very few who have been allowed inside, to see it and live it up close and personal.

Lt. Col. Royal Mortenson says he feels lucky to have left Iraq with all the men he brought into that war zone. I know from watching firsthand that luck comes to those who work hard for it. These Marines are just that and more.

The 2/8 is the example of what all Americans should hope for when the nation calls for military action.

1

Beginnings

The counsel of the LORD stands forever, the plans of His heart to all generations. Blessed is the nation whose God is the LORD, the people He has chosen as His own inheritance.

—PSALM 33:11-12

A Marine believes in his God, in his Country, in his Corps, in his buddies, and in himself.

—GEN. CARL E. MUNDY, USMC, FROM *LEADING MARINES*

Marines undergo a personal transformation at recruit training. There they receive more than just superb training, they are ingrained with a sense of service, honor, and discipline.

—FROM *LEADING MARINES*

FROM THE MOMENT HE TOOK command of the Second Battalion-Eighth Marines (2/8) in December 2001, Lt. Col. Royal Mortenson began to develop an undeniable sense that he and his battalion would be called upon to help fight the war on terrorism. The September 11 attacks on the World Trade Center in New York City and the Pentagon in Washington, D.C., were barely three months old, and America was already heavily engaged in Afghanistan. U.S. Marine Corps units had been brought into the combat there and had performed extremely well. It was just a matter of time, Mortenson thought, before he and 2/8 would likewise be engaged.

Leading troops in combat to defend the United States was the role of a lifetime for a career officer like Mortenson. The Marine Corps has approximately 175,000 active-duty Marines but only eighteen infantry battalions. Mortenson was in command of one of the more storied units. Nicknamed "America's Battalion," this 900-man unit has a proud history that includes the battle of Tarawa in the Pacific in World War II; several rotations in Beirut, Lebanon, from 1981 to 1983; and the rescue of American students and removal of Cuban forces from Grenada in 1983. Actor-director Clint Eastwood even made a movie, titled *Heartbreak Ridge* (1986), based on 2/8's exploits in Grenada.

Commanding an infantry battalion was a perfect fit for Mortenson. He was a nineteen-year veteran when he assumed command and well-educated, as are all U.S. military officers. He had earned a bachelor's and a master's degree and graduated from the Marine Command and Staff College. He was also a graduate of the School of Advanced Warfighting, which provides an extra year of study after Command and Staff College and consists of advanced coursework in the operational level of war, including the study and visitation of classic battles and battlefields.

Decisive, strong-voiced, focused, thoughtful, and physically fit, he was considered by his men, both officers and enlisted, to be an excellent battalion commander (BC). There was a true, heartfelt and unanimous sense of confidence in and praise for his abilities and leadership expressed by every 2/8 Marine interviewed for this book. It is no stretch to state that his Marines truly loved him as their BC. His superiors also considered him to be a very capable and charismatic leader.

Unlike some officers, Mortenson thoroughly enjoys the responsibilities of line command. His strong blend of leadership skills, warfare knowledge, vision, objectivity, aggressiveness, and communication and administration skills are balanced by pragmatism. He leads by example. He demands a lot from his men but is never unfair and does not play favorites. He has succeeded partly because of the mentoring that senior Marine officers have provided, and he in turn works at mentoring his men. His philosophy of command includes statements such as, "It is fine for the Marine to be able to run three miles in eighteen minutes, but it is better to be able to run one mile in seventeen minutes carrying a wounded Marine on your back."

The normal course of events in the U.S. military requires constant recruitment and training. Newly assigned enlisted personnel first must be found and then prepared to replace the experienced, highly trained veterans leaving the service. Mortenson and 2/8 would see dozens of their best-trained infantrymen leave the battalion as their four-year hitches were completed. During the winter of 2002 and into the spring of that year, 2/8 would be receiving a lot of young, inexperienced Marines. Mortenson, as BC, would need to integrate and train these young recruits quickly. But he wasn't worried about that. The young men he would be receiving might be inexperienced, but they all would be Marines.

Formed more than 200 years ago, the United States Marine Corps has earned a sterling reputation as a military organization unsurpassed in its ability to transform young civilians into military personnel. Enlisting men and women from varied and typically unpretentious backgrounds, the Marine Corps forges them into warriors of the highest character and skill. The Marines have a unique process for carrying out this transformation process. It is called "boot camp." Other services use the term "basic training," which lasts six to nine weeks. But for those who want to become Marines, the term is boot camp. It lasts thirteen weeks. After those weeks of intense physical and mental training under the tough, no-nonsense Marine Corps drill instructors, the transformation is achieved.

Our son, Lcpl. David Thomas, was in many ways representative of the young men who enter the Marines after high school to become infantrymen. In school he had done fairly well in courses he liked, yet struggled with those he didn't like—math and science in his case. He enjoyed being outdoors, and he grew up playing sports—mostly ice hockey, football, and track. He was a good athlete and at times played very well. Overall, however, he wasn't always focused. For David—and for every other recruit—the Marine Corps would permanently change that.

David did have some advantages over other recruits upon heading into boot camp in late August 2001. First, he had enlisted in the Marines' delayed-entry program during high school. This had given him some exposure in his senior year to the in-your-face, brutally honest approach of Marine sergeants. His recruiter, Staff Sgt. Timothy Ward, did a fine job of starting the process of transformation and demonstrating commitment.

Second—and more important—David had a significant spiritual and moral advantage: he believed in Jesus Christ. From his birth, his mother, Pam, and I have regularly taught him the Scriptures, prayed for him and tried to instill in him a Christian worldview. Many times as parents we felt our efforts were failing. There were the times of his inconsistent grades in school and the occasional trouble he would get into.

However, even if we were unsure of his future success, the Lord wasn't. Several times during David's last year at home, the Holy Spirit prompted us to encourage and challenge David. As our family laid hands on him and prayed over him the night before he left for boot camp, we had an overwhelming sense from the Lord that he would see significant combat during his time in the Corps. We told him what we were sensing, and the Lord continued leading us to speak over him. We stated that God would protect him and even cause him to prosper in difficult times if he committed his heart to follow the Lord. God said He would also protect those with David but that it would be up to David to make the commitment.

It didn't take long for David to make that pledge. It came during his nighttime bus ride to Parris Island, South Carolina—site of the Marines' East Coast boot camp. As he nervously rode along, staring into the pitch black night, unable to see much of anything and experiencing a growing sense of foreboding, David prayed to the Lord. "I knew I needed the Lord to help get me through this," he recalled later.

Early during boot camp, David wrote a letter to his mother and me in which he described an especially tough day. Boot camp isn't all physical activity and basic infantry-skills training. Marines also have regular classroom lectures, which include a lot of Marine Corps history. The courses help the new recruits build a sense of continuity with Marines who have gone before them. They learn an esprit de corps unlike that instilled by any other branch of military service. One afternoon after a class, David's company went for a five-mile run. When the drill instructors began to ask questions on the just-completed lecture, David answered a question incorrectly. Off he went to the infamous "pit"—a flea-infested sand pit—for 45 minutes of push-ups and sit-ups. The temperature was 95 degrees, with 90 percent humidity.

When he rejoined his company, they had already begun rifle-handling drills. David proceeded to mess up on this because he had missed the beginning instructions. Off he went to the pit again for another forty-five minutes of push-ups and sit-ups. "I was never so sweaty and hungry in my life," he wrote. "I ate dinner in about thirty seconds."

As she read his letter, Pam fought back tears, saying, "My poor baby." I just laughed. "How can you laugh at this?" she asked me tearfully. "Look, honey," I replied, "if this is the worst thing that happens to him during his time in the Corps, that's not so bad! They taught David in one afternoon what we couldn't do in eighteen years—they taught him to focus when he doesn't feel like it! I'll bet you he'll never have trouble again with his concentration." Sure enough, he learned to focus and did well for the rest of boot camp, as did his platoon. They graduated as the honor platoon in the company.

A couple of weeks after David started boot camp, Muslim fanatics attacked New York and Washington with hijacked airliners. The purpose of David's calling was now perfectly clear to him and to us. He and his fellow Marine recruits would be trained and raised up to wage war against evil, cowardly, and deceived terrorists and those who supported them. September 11 caused a sharpening in the attitudes of almost every recruit. Everyone knew their purpose, and the drills became crisper, more vigorous, more focused. These recruits were highly motivated.

The high point of boot camp, the "crucible," came about a week before graduation day. This is a fifty-four-hour, nonstop combat simulation in which Marines must be in full gear and will get only about two or three hours of sleep the entire time. It rained heavily during David's crucible, which made the simulation even more realistic and demanding. Nearly every recruit completed the course and was treated to the "warrior's breakfast," the best meal these young men had during their time at Parris Island. Officially they were now Marines.

The drill instructors treated them differently for that last week, showing them a much greater sense of camaraderie but not letting go of the "rich" and funny language Marine sergeants are known for. For example, before family visitation began on the Thursday before Friday graduation, S. Sgt. Liddle of David's company came into the barracks bright and early and barked: "Today your [expletive] parents will be here! No swearing!"

A strong sense of excitement and patriotism was evident among the many hundreds of family members, wives, and girlfriends attending the graduation ceremony. Everyone knew these young men were destined to become America's front-line defense in the war on terrorism.

After boot camp, Marine infantrymen are sent to the School of Infantry (SOI)—either at Camp Geiger, North Carolina, for East Coast recruits or at Camp Pendleton, California, for West Coast recruits. This school builds upon the basic infantry knowledge learned in boot camp. Skills developed and honed include infantry patrols, urban warfare techniques, jungle fighting, weapons and weapons systems, and enemy weapons and tactics. They also begin training with other Marine infantry specialists who handle and fire mortars, heavy machine guns, grenade launchers, and anti-armor rockets.

While David was home on leave preparing to depart for SOI, the Lord instructed me to tell him to pay special attention to the urban-warfare training he would receive. He was going to need these skills down the road in combat, I believed. David did very well in SOI and learned the urban-warfare techniques thoroughly. For the infantryman, urban combat poses, by far, the greatest chance of becoming a casualty, meaning killed, wounded, or missing in action. At one time, protracted urban fighting resulted in casualty rates as high as seventy-five percent. Since the Persian Gulf War of 1991, however, the Marines have made it a priority to improve their tactics, techniques, and procedures (TTPs) of urban fighting.

Today the Marine Corps trains for urban warfare more stringently than at any other time in its history. Thus, Marines are better at it than ever before. This translates into a significantly reduced chance of taking casualties while greatly increasing the risk to the enemy. The Corps' hard work to improve TTPs would later pay big dividends in sparing American lives during the 2003 war against Saddam Hussein.

A core belief espoused by the Marines is, "Every Marine a Rifleman." The Corps turns this belief into reality by requiring each of its Marines, other than infantrymen, to attend three weeks of Marine Combat Training (MCT). This school, similar to but shorter than the SOI, builds upon the lessons of boot camp. It creates a level of proficiency in every Marine to function at a basic infantry level under realistic combat conditions. The combination of this belief and training has helped turn the tide in many battles in Marine Corps history—as support personnel were organized and thrust into a fray to replace losses or to help hold a line of defense. MCT would once again prove to be a major factor in minimizing casualties in the 2003 war against Iraq.

The modern Marine rifle company packs quite a wallop. It carries much more firepower than even ten or twenty years ago, in both the amount of ordnance and the lethal quality of its weapons systems. Today, a rifle company comprises three rifle platoons, typically of thirty to forty men each; an additional weapons platoon with another forty or so Marines; and a small headquarters section. Every third Marine in the rifle platoons carries a squad automatic weapon (SAW) light machine gun. The other Marines carry M-16s, half with M203 grenade launchers attached. Several men in each platoon carry an AT4 anti-armor rocket, which is much more deadly than the Russian-designed Rocket Propelled Grenades (RPGs) that we hear mentioned so frequently. The weapons platoon Marines carry the M240 Golf 7.62 mm machine gun, heavier SMAW anti-armor rockets, and 60 mm mortars.

Often, a Combined Anti-Armor Anti-Tank (CAAT) section will be assigned to an infantry company. This unit includes four

Humvees equipped with heavy M2 "deuce" .50-caliber machine guns, TOW anti-tank missiles, and the awesome Mark 19 (MK-19) weapon. The MK-19 is a 40 mm, grenade-firing machine gun that can be mounted in the Humvees or on a ground tripod, as can the deuce .50-caliber machine gun. This all translates into a rifle company of 130 to 170 highly trained Marines loaded for bear.

It was at SOI that David first formed many friendships with fellow Marines. Only one Marine—Lcpl. Eric Ross—had been with David in both platoon and company since boot camp. David met several Marines in SOI who became fast friends. They all would eventually serve together in their assigned infantry battalion. These included Lcpls. Brad Ruetschi and Mike Torres. David, Ross, and Ruetschi all look like the ideal Marine: they are six feet or taller, 210 pounds or more. Torres is smaller in stature, no more than 150 pounds, but nobody wanted to mess with him. He grew up amid difficult circumstances in Bronx, New York, and became a Golden Gloves boxing champion. He was good enough to think of trying out for the Marine Corps boxing team. Every Marine infantryman is well-schooled in martial arts and can handle themselves quite well, but once in a while you get one like Torres who can literally knock your lights out in no time flat and think nothing of it. This combination of ability and attitude in Marines like him would prove beneficial, sometimes in unexpected ways, during Operation Iraqi Freedom.

Upon graduation from SOI in April 2002, David, Ross, Ruetschi, and Torres all received prime assignments: they joined Mortenson and the 2/8 at Camp Lejeune, North Carolina. All four of them were assigned to the same rifle company—Golf. The 2/8 includes two other rifle companies, Echo and Fox, and a weapons company and a headquarters and service (H&S) company for a total of five companies in the battalion. In addition, there is the command and control element in the battalion, which consists of the BC, the executive officer (XO), staff personnel including the operations officer (S3) and his assistants, the intelligence officer (S2) with his assistants, and communications specialists.

The weapons company of an infantry battalion possesses the heaviest and most lethal weapons systems in the battalion. It packs heavy 81 mm mortars; more deuce .50-caliber machine guns; several two-man Javelin anti-tank missile teams; and the CAAT platoon, which comprises four sections of four Humvees each, for a total of sixteen, each loaded with MK-19s, deuces and TOW missiles. In addition, the weapons companies of every infantry battalion in the Marine Corps include a platoon of the legendary Marine scout-snipers. The scout-sniper platoon has a normal complement of nine two-man scout-sniper teams. The H&S company contains administrative and service Marines, such as clerks, mechanics, medical personnel—who include Navy corpsmen affectionately called "docs" by the Marines—and logistics specialists who manage the battalion's "log train." The log train is made up of all the trucks and other vehicles carrying the food, water, fuel, and ammunition that keep the battalion running.

Over about a two-week stretch in April 2002, David, Ross, Ruetschi, and Torres were joined by several more SOI graduates who would become good buddies. Lcpls. Dameon Rodriguez, Miguel Noriega, John Cain, and Mishawn Holt all joined 2/8 Golf company as infantrymen. Pfc. Joe Randolfi would join the weapons platoon with Golf later in December. This group of young Marines came from diverse backgrounds. Rodriguez and Noriega grew up streetwise in urban Los Angeles; Cain is a "good ol' boy" from Oklahoma; Holt was raised in Baltimore; and Randolfi came from Tampa, Florida. Most of these young men are dedicated Christians. Noriega's parents are evangelists.

Their weapons assignments were mostly the M-16 rifle or the SAW light machine gun. David, Ross, Torres, and Holt all carried the SAW. The others carried M-16s, except for Randolfi, who was a M240 Golf machine gunner. Golf company totaled about 130 men, although a fully staffed infantry company without any supporting attachments could carry as many as 165. There are situations wherein the Marines deliberately field "undersized" but thoroughly trained units in order to avoid adding green Marines to a seasoned unit. For combat units like these, the benefit of Marines being trained and working as a team is more important than sheer numbers of personnel. A battalion commander's desire is, given ample training time, to have a smaller well-trained unit than a larger less trained, fully staffed unit. Extensive training builds much better cohesiveness within the unit. This fact ultimately pays big dividends in combat. A well-trained 130-man company will whip a much larger, less cohesive unit every time.

Being assigned to a Marine infantry battalion is the real deal. Their mission is clear and focused. They will deploy anywhere in the world to protect Americans and America's interests, and will be the first infantry units to fight if combat becomes necessary. If called into combat, their sole purpose is to destroy the enemy's forces, which they will gladly do without apology. They are first and foremost warriors. Most young Marine Corps officers when first commissioned desire to become infantry officers and command men in combat. That's why most join the Marines in the first place.

However, even within the Marines fewer than one in five officers are selected for infantry service. To be selected is both an honor and a calling. It may be hard for many civilians to understand that someone might actually want to lead men into battle or that these men are so willing to fight. But there is no uncertainty about this with Marines. In the Marine Corps, you are either in infantry, or you support the infantry.

To successfully command a battalion requires seasoned, capable officers who believe in the mission and the vision of the BC. Mortenson helped pull together what would prove to be a superb group of company commanders and staff officers.

The battalion XO was Maj. Julian "Dale" Alford, a veteran of almost every Marine combat deployment since the late 1980s. Alford is taller than most Marines and has the size and physique of a football running back. Cool under fire, with a Southern drawl and chewing tobacco in his gums, he loves leading Marines in combat and possesses the great quality of knowing how to get things done under the duress of battle. The 2/8 Marines who worked with him and for him expressed nothing but love and admiration for him and his leadership skills. Like Mortenson, his ability to communicate with his Marines is exceptional. He is also a keen judge of the skills and abilities of his men. Originally from Georgia, he is secure enough in his calling not to try to downplay his so-called redneck image (his call sign within 2/8 was "Rebel").

It is hard to imagine anyone looking more the part of a Marine infantry officer than Alford.

The battalion S3 was Maj. Robert Fulford. Fulford had been promoted to major and S3 after proving his mettle as Echo rifle company CO for 2/8, running counter-insurgency operations against Albanian militia in Kosovo earlier in 2001. He is a graduate of the U.S. Naval Academy, the son of four-star Marine general Carlton Fulford—former deputy commander of all U.S. forces in Europe—and the grandson of a Baptist minister. Fulford made a personal commitment to Jesus Christ as a boy. Every morning without fail since the ninth grade, he has read a chapter from the Bible. He maintains this discipline even in combat deployments. He learned the power of prayer during the Persian Gulf War in 1991, when his father commanded the Seventh Marine Regiment in combat. Soft-spoken, yet possessing an underlying intensity, Fulford comes across as a very intelligent man who speaks precisely and doesn't waste words. It doesn't take long to figure out this man truly loves the Lord.

The battalion S2 was Capt. John Robert Dupree. Also a veteran of the Persian Gulf War, he had started his Marine Corps career in the enlisted ranks as a .50-caliber machine-gunner. Taking advantage of the GI Bill, he earned a bachelor's in psychology from The Citadel in 1994. Today a committed Christian, Dupree got serious about his walk with the Lord in college and became involved with the Episcopal Church. In addition to his training and deployments as an intelligence officer, he has also commanded a scout-sniper platoon.

Whereas the XO, S2, and S3 officers advise the BC on military options and how to implement his vision, Chaplain Don Rogers—the battalion chaplain—believed his role was, in part, to advise the BC on the morally right thing to do. Like all military chaplains, Rogers is well-educated. He earned a bachelor's degree and master of divinity from Southeastern Baptist Theological Seminary. Unlike most chaplains, however, Rogers started his career as a USMC reservist and trained as a combat engineer, which he thoroughly enjoyed. Combat engineers are in many ways "super grunts," adept in both infantry and demolition techniques. Rogers has been committed to Jesus Christ since age fifteen. God eventually led him to enter the Navy chaplaincy program, and Rogers requested service with the Marine Corps. He joined 2/8 in October 2002.

The five company commanders in 2/8 all were young men in their thirties. They all hold bachelor's degrees—some from military colleges, others from state universities.

Capt. Kevin Yeo led Echo Company. Yeo had spent six years as an enlisted infantryman before deciding to go back to college. He became an officer in 1994, joined 2/8 in 1999, and assumed command of Echo Company in July 2002. Echo Company developed a reputation under Yeo's soft-spoken but hard-driving leadership for being in top physical condition, always well-drilled, and thoroughly trained. His mild manner belies his observant and thoughtful ways. He always seems to be one or two steps ahead of everyone in his anticipation and thinking. He was raised in a Christian home and has a strong belief in the power of prayer.

Capt. Timothy R. Dremann commanded Fox Company. The son of a retired Marine officer and Vietnam veteran, Dremann knew he wanted to be a Marine from the time he was eleven years old. Looking younger than his thirty-one years, he had eight years of infantry officer experience by the time he joined 2/8 in May 2002. His previous assignments included a Parris Island company CO and an XO at drill instructor school. Precise, well-organized and masterful with infantry tactics, he also has the impeccable manners of a traditional, Southern-raised officer and gentleman. Upon joining 2/8 he also had a strong conviction that the battalion would see action. As a regular church attendee and a man of prayer, he would preach "family" to Fox Company. "We developed a strong sense of genuinely caring for each other, like brothers," he said.

Capt. Brian Ross was also an eight-year veteran when he assumed command of Golf Company in May 2002. Born and raised in Alaska, he was attracted to the Marines while in high school. The junior ROTC instructor, James McBroom—a retired Marine Corps master sergeant—had positively influenced him. His infantry assignments also included stints as a recruiting company CO and an assistant director of drill instructor school. The men of Golf Company quickly grew to respect his tactical skills. "He really knows his stuff," David would say. Ross is a discerning judge of his men, able to accurately assess character and temperaments, a CO who always seems to make the correct call on which platoon or squad would best handle specific tasks. He is Roman Catholic by faith and a regular church attendee. He too believed 2/8 would be sent into combat long before it actually happened. "I knew even before I checked into 2/8 that the battalion would see combat," he would recall.

Capt. Benjamin Luciano, affectionately called "Looch" by fellow officers, commanded Weapons Company. In this role, Luciano had two major responsibilities: fire support coordinator for the battalion, and administrative oversight of the various heavy mortar, machine gun, CAAT platoon, and scout-snipers in the battalion. As fire support coordinator, he was responsible to coordinate the fire from regimental and division assets such as field artillery as well as air strikes within the battalion sector. Luciano is a powerfully built man; one might mistake him for a football linebacker if he wasn't wearing his cammies. He was raised Roman Catholic and is a good friend of Chaplain Rogers. His faith would develop while in 2/8 to such a degree that he would have absolutely no doubt that the Lord was watching over the battalion.

Capt. Jim Ryans assumed command of H&S company in October 2002. He joined 2/8 in December 2001 as Fox Company CO. Ryans started his Marine Corps career in 1988 in the enlisted ranks as a radio technician, then took advantage of the Corps' BOOST program (Broaden Opportunity for Officer Selection and Training). BOOST is a terrific program designed to bring up to academic standard aspiring Marines who have performed well and want to attend college to become officers. It is particularly helpful for Marines who, for whatever reason, weren't well-prepared for college after graduating from high school. The three basic areas of study in BOOST are math, science, and English.

"I started in the beginning of the program with simple vocabulary words, and at the end of 10 months I was writing research papers," Ryans said. "I started out with simple math, and when I left I was doing calculus."

Because of BOOST, Ryans won an NROTC scholarship and graduated in 1995 with a degree in physics. His analytical training has led him to combine an interesting set of beliefs about the Christian faith. He describes himself as a "Pentecostal Free-Will Baptist." He also credits the Lord with saving his marriage. His wife is a former Marine officer. As an infantry officer, Ryans gained his first combat experience as a rifle platoon commander with the First Battalion-Eighth Marines during a noncombatant evacuation operation (NEO) in Albania in 1997. Much of the fire was random, but it was still a dangerous situation. "People were shooting at us," he recalled.

It is a fact that the U.S. military has a higher percentage of Christians, especially among officers, than the general population in America. According to Capt. Dupree, a strong majority of Marine Corps officers are Christians. Approximately half of them are Roman Catholic and half are Protestant. Even so, 2/8 had an exceptionally high number of believers, especially among the officers. Capt. Yeo's wife, Andrea, described this truth, saying: "With virtually all the 2/8 officers being believers, this was the first time we'd ever seen this in Kevin's eighteen years in the Corps." God was up to something good with 2/8.

A key to the success of Marine infantry units lies in the platoon officers, senior battalion and company NCOs, and platoon and squad sergeants. These are the men responsible for turning orders into action. David, Rodriguez, Ross, Ruetschi, Noreiga, Torres, Cain, and Holt all were part of Second Platoon originally, which was commanded by 2nd Lt. Fitzsimmons. Three squads of seven to nine men each made up Second Platoon. David and Torres were part of First Squad, led by Sgt. Campbell, who was highly respected by his men for his tactical and leadership skills.

Most Marine battalions have several memorable senior NCOs, and 2/8 is certainly no exception. The senior NCOs in Golf company were 1st Sgt. Beith, and Gunnery Sgt. "Gunny" Sweeney. First Sgt. Beith pretty much played the role of a good guy, overseeing his enlisted men with a good deal of care and concern. Gunny Sweeney played the tough guy, and he was perfect for the role.

Sweeney stands about six feet-four inches, weighs in around 215 pounds (of pure muscle), and possesses a mean-looking countenance. A former drill instructor, he would straighten up any Marine in his company when he saw something he didn't like. "Everybody, even the platoon lieutenants, were scared of him," David said. Even Sweeney's first name wasn't readily known. "You're not supposed to know Gunny Sweeney's first name," David said.

The senior NCO for Fox Company was 1st Sgt. Howard Gatewood. If there was ever a man who looks like the perfect Marine, Gatewood would be him. Standing six feet-one inch and packing 215 pounds of chiseled muscle, he looks 20 pounds heavier than his actual weight. Before joining the Marines in August 1985, Gatewood was a scholarship football player at Alcorn State University in Mississippi. He has a thick neck and square jaw and speaks in a firm voice. Gatewood doesn't waste words in conversation. His physical appearance and traits give real meaning to the word "intensity." A former drill instructor, Gatewood spent a significant amount of his career performing combat engineering assignments. He fought in Operation Desert Storm in 1991, performing the dangerous work of clearing minefields.

First Sgt. Hawkins was Echo Company's senior NCO. He has an outgoing personality and will respectfully speak his mind to senior officers without mixing words. A dedicated Christian and family man, Hawkins was equally as effective or more so as any first sergeant, while somehow still managing to be liked by all the Marines in his company. At six feet-three inches and a muscular 210 pounds, he will run and "hump it" with the fittest of Marines. As a combat veteran who was cool under fire, Hawkins would lead his men from the front in battle in Operation Iraqi Freedom.

The most senior NCO in the battalion was Sgt. Maj. Thorne, whose office at Camp Lejeune was located just around the corner from Mortenson's. With a ramrod straight walk and bulldog demeanor, Thorne was all business, but he loved being among his fellow enlisted Marines. Making rounds, even in battle, he would always inquire how his men were doing. He enjoyed seeing to it that his company and platoon sergeants got what they needed to do their job. When agitated, Thorne was likely to include lots of expletives in his speech, but you got the point very well.

Another memorable NCO was 1st Sgt. Squires, the senior sergeant in Luciano's Weapons Company. Squires has a few unique methods for transferring Marine Corps wisdom to young enlisted men. Standing a wiry five feet-ten inches, possessing abundant energy and speaking with somewhat of a high-pitched yet piercing voice out of the side of his mouth, he would freely dispense his advice, especially when asked to address the battalion immediately before or after a weekend of liberty.

"In case you've forgotten, drugs are still illegal" he would say, then add: "I don't know why you all can't remember this! The Good Lord will punish the wicked! If you smoke weed, the Good Lord will use me to punish you!" As for married Marines, he would advise, "You guys who go home and think you're going to hit your wife. Stop this [expletive]! If you want to fight, go to a bar and get in a fight with another Marine!"

But Squires would save his best for a one-on-one session with young Marines in his company who did manage to get in trouble, usually over a weekend. John Cain described one such eventful meeting.

"He calls you into his office, with nobody else, just you and him, and he closes the door. Without saying anything about your infraction, he calmly turns his head toward a large portrait of Chesty Puller [a legendary Marine general and hero of World War II and the Korean War] hanging on the wall, and begins a soliloquy: 'Well, Chesty, I need your help here. I got this young Marine here, and he's messed up real good. I don't know whether I should bust him rank, or just beat the stuffing out of him. I need your help, now, Chesty. Talk to me! Talk to me, Chesty!' And he goes on like this for a while. It scares the daylights out of you—you don't know what he's going to do!" Most young Marines straighten up after just one visit with Squires.

Commanding such a diverse group of some 900 personalities as Mortenson did, it is not difficult to see the challenging task he had in shaping and preparing 2/8 for combat. It was a responsibility as shall be seen that he executed extremely well.

2

PREPARATION

It is God who arms me with strength, and makes my way perfect.
He makes my feet like the feet of deer, and sets me on my high
places. He teaches my hands to make war, so that my arms can
bend a bow of bronze.

—PSALM 18:32-34

But now indeed there are many members, yet one body.

—1 CORINTHIANS 12:20

Service with the Marine Corps means service with a team. Everything that the Marine Corps does is a team effort. Every unit from
the Marine expeditionary force down to the fire team is organized
into a team—a group of highly select, well-trained Marines all
pointed to one objective.

—FROM *LEADING MARINES*

S INCE TAKING COMMAND OF 2/8 in December 2001, Lt.
Col. Mortenson believed very strongly the battalion had
a destiny in combat and that it would be up to him to
prepare his men thoroughly. Since September 11 the battalion
had been on the contingency list of forces to fight the war on
terrorism. Mortenson was certain that at some point he would
be leading 2/8 into harm's way. It was an opportunity he rel-
ished and had been preparing for his entire career. He had seen
during his time examples of good battalion training as well as
examples of incomplete and somewhat disjointed training. He
was determined to develop and execute a training strategy and
plan that would incorporate the best of what he had learned and

take advantage of all that the Corps could offer a BC.

The fundamental organization of the Marine Corps for conducting missions is called MAGTF (Marine Air-Ground Task Force). All Marine fighting units, whether a 900-man battalion or a 50,000-man Marine Expeditionary Force, are built and trained within the MAGTF organization. Marine infantry battalions serve as a ground element in MAGTF and are combined with other elements to create a balanced, self contained, scalable, and versatile combined-arms expeditionary force. Full MAGTF units include infantry, armor, artillery, reconnaissance, combat engineering, air-strike, air-transport, command, and supply elements. The Corps forward deploys its supporting units. Thus, an infantry unit can call for artillery or close air support, and typically within a few minutes ordnance will be landing on a target. Such a synergistic approach to fighting is one reason why the Marines have repeatedly throughout their history defeated much larger enemy forces in combat.

Mortenson knew that constant training would be a key to fully preparing his men. He went to work and developed an eighteen-month plan that called for 2/8 to deploy for training approximately every three months. He manipulated as best he could the higher level regimental and divisional training schedules to turn his plan into reality. His battalion plan included quarterly training plans and required his staff and company commanders to create quarterly and weekly plans for their units that supported the battalion training goals. His fully integrated training plan linked the training with personnel changes, logistical support, and fiscal budgets. "It was the ultimate team concept," Mortenson said.

The training schedule was busy. It started with five weeks at CAX (Combined Arms Exercise) at 29 Palms, California, in February 2002. CAX is realistic, live-fire combat training, with integrated units working together within parameters of MAGTF doctrine against mock opposing forces. CAX was followed by a three-week deployment to Spain in May to participate in Dynamic Mix 2002, the biennial combined-forces NATO exercise. This was followed by four weeks of mountain training in the Sierra Nevada Mountains of California in September. The return trip to CAX was slated for January 2003. Between the deployments was a constant stream of company- and battalion-level field operations at Camp Lejeune.

For David and his buddies, from the time they arrived at Golf Company in April 2002 the training was incessant. Their first month saw Golf receive helicopter and air-assault qualification. Riding and jumping out of the huge CH53E Super Stallions was a blast for them. While Golf received air-assault training, Echo Company trained in mechanized vehicles, and Fox Company trained for amphibious assaults. Physical training (PT)—lots of running and calisthenics—was a regular early morning event. David and Eric spent a lot of their free time pumping iron in the weight room.

The first deployment for David was Dynamic Mix 2002 in Spain. The battalion had been placed organizationally under Col. John C. Coleman's Sixth Regiment. In addition to 2/8, the other units deployed included the Second Tank Battalion; Second Battalion Tenth Marines, which is an artillery battalion; a company of light armored reconnaissance (LAR); and a detachment of a Combat Service Support Element (CSSE) for supporting the regiment. For David and his buddies, it was exciting to experience large-unit operations with thousands of fellow Marines and other soldiers. It was also eye-opening for them to see the relative obsolescence and sub-par training of the Spanish Army. Although the Spanish snipers and Special Operations forces appeared to be capable and professional, the bulk of the regular army was not. Upon his return to Camp Lejeune, David told me, "Dad, if we go to war, you can tell the Spanish Army to stay home!" One treat 2/8 experienced in Spain was a review by the Commandant of the Marine Corps, General James L. Jones, who had flown over. David said later: "That was awesome! Most Marines go through their four-year enlistment and never meet the commandant, and here we are in not even a year and he comes and reviews us! He said, 'You're a good looking bunch of devil dogs,' as he walked past me."

The frequent field ops at Lejeune were essential to building teamwork and honing infantry skills. The young Marines knew this. "We needed to gain familiarity with our fellow platoon team members," David said. "We had to learn how to work together, how to understand what the sergeants and officers really wanted done with their commands, how to react to situations as a team. It took us about three or four months to get really good at working together as a platoon." Likewise, Capt. Ross and his platoon lieutenants and senior NCOs were learning the capabilities and personalities of their men, down to squad and even individual level. From the time David arrived at 2/8 until the end of 2002, Capt. Ross conducted more than twenty field ops at Lejeune with his company, including live fire exercises and drills.

The mountain warfare training at Bridgeport, California, from mid-September to mid-October, was when Mortenson believed the battalion truly came together as a highly capable, smoothly functioning team. The other officers also noticed this. "The mountain training was really good for the squad level and individuals, working together as a team, developing esprit de corps. All the activities—climbing mountains, mountain patrols, rappelling, walking the one-rope bridge—caused them to learn to trust the man to their left and their right" Capt. Ross said.

Capt. Ryans concurred. "Bridgeport jelled the battalion together as one big team," he said. The training was good for enlisted men and officers alike. Major Alford described Bridgeport as "the best training ground for young company commanders." For the young enlisted Marines, it was a terrific experience. "We thought it was indicative of the type of warfare we might see in Afghanistan," David said, adding, "It was fun stuff—cliff assaults, rappelling, top-roping, mountain patrols, fast-roping out of helos—and we got a weekend liberty in Reno!"

One of the anticipated scenarios that 2/8 continually prepared for was nuclear-biological-chemical (NBC) warfare. It was known that Saddam Hussein had already engaged in chemical warfare against the Iranians in the 1980's and had unleashed chemical weapons against the Kurds of northern Iraq, killing thousands. It was also known that terrorist groups such as al-Qaida were seeking NBC capabilities. Capt. Ross was especially keen about continually drilling his men for NBC warfare in the latter half of 2002. "I thought it would be a huge issue over the next six to eight months, and I hammered away at it with my Marines," he said. In addition, Mortenson assigned Golf Company to ensure that 2/8 met the Second Marine Division's NBC "ORE"—Operational Readiness Evaluation, which 2/8 readily passed.

Because of all the focused training, and because events in Iraq were heating up and operations were continuing in Afghanistan by late fall of 2002, most of the men of 2/8 had come to believe that they would be seeing conflict soon. The senior officers were privy to the contingency plans for war with Iraq, and 2/8 was included. Major Fulford recalled that, "It was clear from where the battalion was placed that if there was ever a decision to go to war with Iraq, 2/8 would be part of it."

Contingency plans are typically developed for various scenarios, and one scenario included a regiment-sized ground force from Second Marine Division at Camp Lejeune participating in a war against Saddam Hussein. Initial plans for the ground regiment had selected the Sixth Marines, but personnel changes led to the Second Marine Regiment commanded by Col. Ronald L. Bailey being placed in this contingency. In later discussions with Col. Bailey about these events, it became quite clear that the Lord had been steadily leading Bailey to prepare for this combat command just as He had been doing with Mortenson and 2/8.

Bailey is a very committed Christian, a believer who has attended Sunday church services his entire life. His 8 a.m. daily devotions, usually held with his command chaplain, are a normal part of his everyday schedule. While discussing his commitment to devotions, Bailey later stated, "I don't even allow them to be separate from my military life." If you walk into his office and interrupt his devotional routine, you will be ordered either to join in the study or come back later. An exceptional athlete and boxer who was a 1982 South Carolina Golden Gloves champion, he has held every infantry assignment an officer can have including platoon commander; commands of Rifle, Weapons, and Security Force companies; operations and executive officer positions; and battalion commander, culminating in the command of the Second Marines. He holds a bachelor's degree in biology with minors in chemistry and military science. He earned a master's degree in business administration as well as a master's in international relations and military science.

Before taking command of the Second Marines in July 2002, and even before September 11, Bailey had a sense that during his next assignment as a regimental commander he would likely be called on to lead his unit into combat. He accordingly started to prepare himself for this prospect while still in his role as a J5 Plans Officer in Europe during 2001 and early 2002. "As a plans officer in Europe, I was able to look at all the plans," Bailey later recalled. "They started talking about Operation Iraqi Freedom nine months before I took over Second Marines. It was just a matter of time before our next move would be going into Iraq. I started studying and preparing for it long before."

Part of his disciplined preparation was to discuss fighting tactics with officers who had fought in Desert Storm in 1991. By fall 2002, Bailey had prepared his regiment well, with training that had included the CAX live-fire exercises from July to September. "CAX really meshed the staff," Bailey observed later. "CAX was tremendous preparation that we had as a regiment prior to Operation Iraqi Freedom." One of his infantry battalions, 2/2, had deployed on an MEU assignment, so his regiment needed a third infantry battalion. Bailey had heard of Mortenson, Alford, and Fulford. He had been told good things about 2/8 but had not yet worked with them or the battalion. Soon enough, however, their destinies would converge.

Although the specifics of the planning process were not shared with the enlisted men, the message to prepare for war, especially mentally and spiritually, was getting through. Chaplain Rogers had been told by Chaplain Renard, the Sixth Marines Regimental Command Chaplain, to be "prepared to go to war" when Rogers joined 2/8 in October. This caused Rogers to spend much more time in prayer and Bible reading through the balance of 2002.

David sensed from his own prayer time that the Lord was leading him to focus hard on three key skills during the training: fire and movement, urban warfare, and weaponry. David perfected his knowledge of the SAW. In his words, "I knew it like the back of my hand," in order to deliver the highest possible uptime in operations.

These skills would, in fact, turn out to be the three most important ones he relied upon later in Iraq. In the final weeks of 2002 he didn't concern himself with certain other infantry skills, such as jungle patrols. A reinforcing of what he sensed from God came repeatedly throughout December. "We had a lot of classes in Iraqi climate, geography, and their military, and there aren't any real jungles there," David said. "But even with the classroom instruction, no officer or NCO ever directly stated, 'We're going to Iraq.'"

When the officers of 2/8 would look back on this time, they would to a man appraise the battalion status in two ways: it was superbly trained, and the hand of God was over them. Capt. Luciano stated that 2/8 was "the most prepared" battalion he'd ever been in. Capt. Dupree observed: "Fortunately for us, the Lord had His hand in it, making sure this battalion was strong enough to handle whatever happened to it."

The battalion received Christmas leave starting on December 19, with orders to return by January 5 to make final preparations to leave for CAX training. The political scene between the United States and Iraq had become heated, and words began circulating that 2/8 would not be heading to California in January. "Right before Christmas we heard an inkling that 2/8 wasn't going to CAX, and it looked like something was up," Capt. Ross said. If an omen was needed, Maj. Alford provided it. On three previous occasions he had been part of battalions scheduled for CAX training, and three times his unit had deployed instead to combat—to Panama, to Iraq for Operation Desert Storm, and to Liberia, respectively. The standard joke among the officers of 2/8 became: "Alford's here, so forget CAX. Only combat will do!"

While home on leave, David was calm and relaxed. Believing even before he joined the Marines that he would see combat, he chose not to think about it much while he was home. He expressed a few times his complete confidence in a U.S. victory if war with Iraq came but said little else. On December 26, during a time of prayer, I wrote in my journal what the Holy Spirit had impressed on me to pray. For David, I prayed for God's protection, a clear mind and a heart focused on God. Then the Holy Spirit spoke to me about Iraq. There would be war, He said, 2/8 would go, and it would do very well with few casualties. This was the first hard, insightful sense that God gave our family about these future events, and it brought about a decided change in our daily prayers. The Holy Spirit began leading us daily to pray for the U.S. military, the military commanders, and chain of command—including President Bush, Secretaries Rumsfeld and Powell, the Joint Chiefs, the Commanding General and staff of Central Command, the Marine Corps commanders, and 2/8 officers and sergeants—and David and his buddies. Protection, wisdom, and courage were the primary topics we requested for them. God also instructed us to pray for the Iraqi people, for their protection, and that they would understand the United States meant to help them by removing Saddam Hussein and by assisting in the rebuilding of their country.

While home on Monday, December 30, David received a phone call from a sergeant at battalion headquarters, who stated: "The battalion has been called back early. You are to report in by 1700 this Thursday, January 2. And don't bring your car, you won't be needing it." As he hung up the phone, David excitedly said, "We're going!"

3

DEPLOYMENT

Our soul waits for the Lord; He is our help and our shield. For our heart shall rejoice in Him, because we have trusted in His holy name. Let Your mercy, O Lord, be upon us, just as we hope in You.

—PSALM 33:20-22

Each individual Marine, because of the fighting tradition of the Corps and the toughness of the training, is confident of his own ability and that of his buddies.

—FROM *LEADING MARINES*

THE MIDDLE EAST IS THE primary responsibility of the I Marine Expeditionary Force (I MEF) based at Camp Pendleton, California. However, with large planned engagements such as Operation Desert Storm, I MEF will "invite" major units of II MEF from Camp Lejeune to join in their efforts. Due largely to former Sixth Marines CO, Col. John Coleman, who had become the chief of staff of I MEF, 2/8 had a good reputation within I MEF and had been included all along in contingency plans for a war with Iraq.

Mortenson received orders to deploy 2/8 and on December 30 started the formal process of recalling his men. There were, however, a few unexpected changes to the orders that immediately sent the officers and NCOs into high gear. The contingency plans that had been considered the most likely to be used called for 2/8 to become a fourth infantry battalion in the Seventh Marines and join I MEF; 2/8 would then deploy to theater by air transport. The orders that came through on December 30 requested the entire Second Marine Expeditionary Brigade (II MEB) from Camp Lejeune—roughly 15,000 men, a brigade-sized MAGTF force complete with a full ground Regimental Combat Team (RCT), a Marine Air Group (MAG), a Combat Service Support Element (CSSE), and a Command Element.

Brig. Gen. Richard Natonski would command the II MEB and report to Lt. Gen. James Conway, CO of I MEF. Marine Air Group Twenty-Nine commanded by Col. Milstead would provide the air component of the II MEB. In no surprise to Col. Bailey, his Second Marine Regiment was chosen as the ground element of II MEB and was renamed Regimental Combat Team Two (RCT-2). Because the Second Battalion from the Second Marines was on an MEU deployment, 2/8 was selected to replace 2/2 and was moved into RCT-2 under Bailey.

The three other battalions that 2/8 joined to compose the bulk of RCT-2 were Bailey's First and Third infantry battalions of the Second Marines (1/2 and 3/2) commanded by Lt. Col. Rick Grabowski and Lt. Col. Brent Dunahoe, respectively, and the First Battalion, Tenth Marines (1/10) commanded by Lt. Col. Glenn Starnes. Starnes was an old friend of Mortenson's from their days in Amphibious Warfare School when they were young Captains. Contrasting the infantry battalions, Starnes' 1/10 is an artillery battalion equipped with eighteen powerful 155 mm field guns.

Supporting units within RCT-2 included Company A of the Second Combat Engineer Battalion, Company C of the Second Light Armored Reconnaissance Battalion (2nd LAR), Company A of the Second Reconnaissance Battalion, Company A of the Eighth Tank Battalion, and Company A of the Second Assault Amphibious Battalion. But the biggest change was that the II MEB, including 2/8, would now deploy via U.S. Navy vessels in a task force of amphibious assault ships—and not by air. Two assault ships, the *USS Saipan* and the *USS Kearsarge*, would transport 2/8 to theater.

Mortenson and 2/8 had until January 9, just eleven days, to completely reorganize their logistical plan and ship out.

It was crunch time. Fifteen-hour days or longer became the norm. As might be expected, different men had different reactions to the deployment orders. Dremann, knowing something was up before the Christmas break, had taken the opportunity to prepare his family. He spoke about his likely deployment with his wife and children, and continued the family's normal routine of attending church and saying nightly prayers. From January 3 onward, 2/8 was so busy, Dremann said, that they "were not giving much thought" to where they were going. It was hard on his family, who wished he would spend more time at home before leaving, but he simply could not.

Mortenson, believing this day would come, said he already "had gotten my house in order." In addition, as BC he had spent considerable time in the preceding weeks mentally playing through various combat scenarios.

Despite the rush and long days, Ryans felt very much at ease. "At no point in time did I ever even think that I would not come back," he said. He had a strong sense of peace and conviction from the Holy Spirit—so much so that he told his wife, "I'll let you know if you need to get worried!"

Capt. Ross would later recall: "It's difficult to explain at times. You don't become a Marine infantry company commander to go do a capabilities exercise at Camp Lejeune; it's like training for the Super Bowl—you want to play in the Super Bowl. I knew this was a worthwhile mission, that at some point we were going to have to take care of Saddam Hussein." Ross said he and his family "were praying at every opportunity we had." His wife, Tracy, posted prayers on their refrigerator and recited them often during those hurried days.

For David, it was exciting, a new experience. "We knew our training would be utilized," he said. "Everyone was motivated, everyone was on the ball."

The forward unit from 2/8 led by Maj. Alford departed January 5, and the bulk of the battalion shipped by bus to Norfolk, Virginia, on January 9, right on schedule. Fox, Golf, Weapons, and H&S companies boarded the *USS Saipan*, and Echo Company loaded onto the *USS Kearsarge*. The *Saipan*, commanded by Capt. N.L. Hackney, pulled out of port January 10, a departure that made the news on CNN. The ship proceeded the short distance down to Morehead City, North Carolina, to load cargo. Remaining off the coast of North Carolina for a few days to join up with the *Kearsarge* and the other amphibious ships of II MEB, the brigade departed for Kuwait on January 16.

Life for a Marine aboard amphibious assault ships the size of the *Saipan* and *Kearsarge* is quite good. After the supercarriers, the *Kearsarge* and her sister ships of the LHD class are the largest vessels in the Navy. The LHA class of ships, which includes the *Saipan*, are close behind in size. Each ship is more than 820 feet long and weighs 40,000 tons or more. They provided a stable and comfortable ride for the 1,900 Marines and 1,000 sailors who embarked on them. Even though the two ships are similar size, the newer ships in the *Kearsarge* class can carry significantly more vehicles, weapons, and stores. There are well-equipped gyms on the ships, which saw a lot of use, especially from the transient Marines. The food is good, at least by the standards of 19-year-old servicemen.

While 2/8 deployed, back on the home front God was leading our family into more detailed prayers that would become daily petitions for the next several months. On January 8, I noted in my journal that the Lord was leading us to pray three specific requests:

1. That God would place a triple hedge of protection around David and his fellow Marines; and that no harm would come upon them from the Iraqi military or from friendly or accidental fire, or from a demonic scheme such as frenzied civilians attacking them.

2. That God would keep David's mind focused and sharp—clearly focused on both the things of God and his duties as a Marine.

3. That the favor of God would be on him, his fellow Marines, his chain of command, and with all those he came in contact with.

In addition to these daily prayers, we prayed for the peaceful removal of Saddam Hussein, which throughout the month of January was a frequently stated prayer request in churches and Christian TV and radio shows across America. There was at this time a genuine hope that Saddam would be removed from power without a fight.

The thirty-five-day transit to Kuwait gave the officers of 2/8 plenty of time to continue training exercises, albeit emphasizing mental preparations. Capt. Ross ran a lot of tactical decision games with his officers and NCOs, planning out communication responses to anticipated field actions. Twice a week he met with his platoon lieutenants, who would usually meet once a day with their platoons. The officers also kept everyone informed of the Iraq situation, the status of U.N. inspections, and press releases from President Bush and his administration. "Everyone had their guess as to what would happen," Ross said.

Physical training focused on NBC, first aid, small unit tactics, some live fire off the ship, and regular weapons cleaning and handling drills. The only real excitement during transit came when the ship passed through the Suez Canal. There had been reports that al-Qaida might try to attack the ships in the confined waters of the Suez, so watches were reinforced with machine guns and with AH-1 Cobra attack helicopters flying overhead. Fortunately the Suez passage turned out to be uneventful.

The shipboard training and watches typically required only a few hours per day, so there was plenty of time for the troops to work out, read, relax, sleep, and contemplate the gravity of the situation they would shortly enter. David used his free hours to read through Psalms several times and to spend time in prayer while he lay on his bunk. He specifically asked God to give him a spirit of confidence and a spirit of relaxation, so he would avoid worrying.

Maj. Fulford continued his daily routine of devotions and prayer, and sensed the Holy Spirit giving him extra assurance. Psalm 46:10, "Be still and know that I am God," hit him powerfully. "It took me back to my experience as a college student, when my father went to Gulf War I. At that time I was closer to God than I had ever been, prayerwise," he said.

Ryans continued his regular prayer and Bible reading and was so relaxed he started second guessing himself. *Hey, I need a little more edge,* he thought. At the same time, his desire was to command a rifle company, and a piece of him wrestled with that. Ryans knew that commanding H&S Company well was vitally important if 2/8 was to succeed in any future combat—but infantry officers desire line command. Despite his desire, he kept hearing the Holy Spirit saying, "Be content in all things." This helped him believe God had him exactly where He wanted him.

Chaplain Rogers spent his personal prayer time asking God to protect 2/8, for the Marines to exercise a lot of courage, and for all of them to be focused. Rogers also took the opportunity on board ship to request one-on-one time with Mortenson in his stateroom, to pray with him and for him. "I've never done this before, but, I am your chaplain," Rogers told Mortenson. They met about once a week and continued this practice later while in Kuwait, right up to the start of combat. Rogers also ministered on the *Saipan* to the men of 2/8, through regular Sunday services, and by praying and talking with every man who made a request of him. He handed out Psalm 91 cards, titled "The Soldier's Psalm," to all who attended a prayer service a few days before they disembarked from the *Saipan* in mid-February.

Mortenson was confident that 2/8 would fare very well if called to combat, and he truly was not fearful for his own life. Nevertheless, he sensed he needed to make a stronger commitment to God. Chaplain Peter St. George, a Catholic priest who had been the 2/8 battalion chaplain before Rogers, had been flown onto the *Saipan* to perform confessionals and to hold services. Mortenson took the opportunity to be confirmed into the Catholic faith by St. George.

While the ships carrying II MEB were steaming closer to Kuwait in early February, political events between Saddam Hussein, the United States, and the United Nations continued to escalate. At the home churches of the men of 2/8, and at churches throughout America, there was a growing sense that conflict would soon come, and responsive pastors began calling for prayer and organizing prayer boards and prayer groups. Tens of thousands of military personnel deploying to the Middle East theater had their pictures and prayer requests posted on their church prayer boards. Friends and relatives posted names and pictures in their churches as well, so it was not uncommon for service personnel to have four or five separate churches praying for them by name.

David's picture was on the prayer boards and lists of several other churches in western New York besides his home church, Southtowns Christian Center near Buffalo. These included Lovejoy Gospel Church, where his older sisters and friend Erin attended; Eastern Hills Wesleyan Church, where more friends attended; and two churches attended by work associates of mine. The senior pastor of Lovejoy Gospel Church, Dr. Ron Burgio, really took prayer for the deployed servicemen and servicewomen seriously. Pastor Burgio had a prayer team of seventy church members who prayed daily for him, and he added David's name and those of the other deployed military personnel from the church to the prayer list. From this time, until David returned from Iraq, more than seventy people from just this one church were praying for his protection and favor from God every single day.

John Cain's family in Oklahoma and Arizona also sensed the urge to pray and responded. No less than ten churches of family and friends across America were praying for John by name and for 2/8. In addition to their home church in Oklahoma City were his parents, John and Ruth, and brother-in-law and sister, Jason and Rebecca Redman, attended, there were several other Oklahoma churches praying. John's second sister, Jennifer Peterson, and her husband, James, had believers praying in their home church, Cornerstone Assembly of God and also at a local Calvary Chapel, both in Phoenix, Arizona. Additional churches involved in prayer for John and 2/8 included three Michigan churches, one California church, and one church in Idaho.

Capt. Ross's family also took to prayer. Ross's father in Anchorage, Alaska, arranged a prayer community to hold Ross, Golf Company, and 2/8 up through prayer. The senior Ross had become a big believer in the power of prayer a few years earlier when he had been diagnosed with terminal cancer. He was miraculously healed, and he readily credits answered prayer from God with curing him. Capt. Ross later stated "[My Dad] has continued as a man of prayer ever since. Dozens of believers back in Alaska were praying for me by name."

At our home church of Southtowns Christian Center, Senior Pastor Tommy Smardz openly encouraged the congregation to pray and seek God's favor for U.S. and allied military personnel in prayer. At the 10 a.m. service on Sunday, February 9, more than one month before hostilities started, two parishioners came forward and spoke words to the church that would later prove to be prophetic, meaning timely, and absolutely correct concerning the events that would come to pass.

The first word stated there will be a war with Saddam Hussein, that believers will help bring about the will of God through prayer, and that believers should not trust solely in American military strength but through prayer the victory will come. The second word proclaimed that the call of God is for prayer; and in the coming weeks God will wake some up in the midnight hours to pray, and that diligence in prayer as God leads will be rewarded with His causing the Iraqi enemy to become confused and fearful, so much so they will be incapable of properly functioning as a military unit, and thereby God will spare not only American lives but also Iraqi lives. This word finished by stating this is part of God's plan, beginning with Afghanistan and now Iraq, to remove political leaders who oppose God, who hate Him and have worked against His will and purposes. What many of the Marines of 2/8 had believed for some time was now becoming very clear to family and friends back in America: the United States would fight another war against Saddam Hussein, and it would be a just cause.

On February 16 the naval task force ferrying 2/8 had reached Kuwait, and the battalion disembarked from the *Saipan* and *Kearsarge* by both helicopter and landing craft and set up camp in their assigned sector. Their battalion area in northern Kuwait became a virtual "tent city," covered with large general purpose tents each housing eighteen to twenty Marines. The officers and NCOs quickly began to organize their men for more training.

Capt. Ross ran many battle drills with the nine trucks he was given for Golf Company, figuring out seemingly simple issues like how best to load, unload and fit eighteen Marines with equipment into each truck, and where to place sand bags for protection. They practiced convoy operations, "immediate action drills" (meaning what to do when someone starts shooting at the trucks), land navigation in the desert both day and night including the use of hand held global positioning system (GPS) units, and worked to perfect these techniques and communications that typically weren't addressed back at Camp Lejeune.

In addition, Ross drilled Golf for open desert warfare as seen in Gulf War I, including NBC, with care given to proper fitting of their protective suits, trench clearing, and bunker clearing. David described trench clearing as, "Forty guys would dig a trench, then practice running through it." They became creative in training for urban warfare, practicing their urban patrol techniques back in tent city.

Captains Dremann and Yeo likewise worked to get their rifle companies ready. "We were preparing for a wide spectrum of operations, from unrestrained combat to humanitarian aid to peace enforcement," Dremann said. The battalion did have live fire exercises, though not as many as everyone would have liked, and ran some joint training with Force Recon units, highly trained special operations Marines whose difficult missions make them the Marine Corps version of Special Forces units such as U.S. Army Green Berets and Navy SEALS. David wrote home admiringly of Force Recon, "These guys are no joke!"

Despite the preparations, the men still had a considerable amount of free time, much like they did on the *Saipan* and *Kearsarge*. PT was constant and pickup football games were common. Chaplain Rogers started a daily Bible study in the back of a large tent, water-baptized two men, and even got to preach in a Sunday service. He spent much of his free time among the men, and not surprisingly a lot of Marines came to him to request prayer. Capt. Luciano took time to read the Bible cover to cover and used much of his remaining downtime to talk at length with Chaplain Rogers.

As the days passed into March, David had a growing sense from God that when war did come, victory for the United States would be certain. He also sensed God telling him that no one in his platoon, Second Platoon of Golf Company, would be killed in combat.

Mortenson continued to inspire his men with the same consistent message he had been declaring to them since he took command of 2/8: do the right thing; be the best man you can be, and you will be a good Marine; character counts; pick up your fellow Marine; be guided by moral character and strength of will. He believed, for the most part, that the troops of 2/8 had come to believe in these principles. To these words he added a short, purposeful message: the way home is north, through Baghdad.

At RCT-2 headquarters in Kuwait, Col. Bailey was preparing both his staff and himself for war. A critical component for Bailey was to continually develop and maintain his relationship with the Lord, which included regular times of prayer with his command chaplain, Chaplain Gordon Ritchie, and with his regimental sergeant, Sgt. Maj. Eddie Evans, who also was a devout Christian. In every infantry command he has had, Bailey has developed strong relationships with his chaplains.

Bailey had a twofold purpose for doing so. First, he believed it was good for his own heart, soul, mind, and body. Second, Bailey liked to use his chaplains to help get a sense of the rhythm of the command. "It is a chance to hear my chaplain talk, to hear how he's thinking and what he's saying to my Marines, and to get feedback on my Marines' actions and thoughts," Bailey later explained. During Operation Iraqi Freedom, Bailey and Ritchie would sit to talk, meditate, and pray whenever they had downtime. They would use a daily devotional book originally published during World War II—*Strength for Service*—which they found just as current for their needs in 2003 as believers did sixty years before.

Sgt. Maj. Evans was also a godsend for Bailey. Bailey and Evans had previously worked together when Bailey was a battalion commander. Evans was completely dedicated to his regimental commander. "Eddie Evans was with me everywhere. He never left my side during Operation Iraqi Freedom," Bailey stated later. "I received great counsel from him."

Col. Bailey had also begun to receive large volumes of letters and care packages from his home church, from the churches of family members and friends across America, and even from elementary schools. This outpouring of support from home became the norm for RCT-2 Marines. Caring Americans were writing Bailey's men and supplying snacks such as granola and power bars, hard candy, shaving cream and razors, tooth brushes and toothpaste, soap, shampoo, and baby wipes. The baby wipes were especially valued by the troops. Unable to shower very often while in Kuwait—and not at all after the war started—the Marines used the baby wipes to cleanse themselves as best they could. With their letters of encouragement from home and the tangible goodies, Americans were providing invaluable comfort and support to the Marines of Operation Iraqi Freedom.

Chaplain Ritchie and the battalion chaplains of RCT-2 made the best of the available spartan facilities while in Kuwait. Working with chaplains Don Rogers of 2/8, Kevin Norton of 1/10, Dan Hoedl of 1/2, and Brian White of 3/2, Ritchie set up formal Sunday church services at Camp Shoop, using one of the large chow-hall tents. Each Sunday the Chaplains ran two services, one Catholic, one Protestant. Both services were packed to capacity every Sunday, with more than 600 Marines attending the two services. The chaplains shared the preaching duties. Being able to attend a Mass or service is something taken for granted in America, but for these servicemen facing the prospect of war there was no better use of their time. Calling on the Lord in this difficult time with hundreds of fellow Marines brought immense comfort and a stronger sense of camaraderie to each person.

As February pressed into March, some of the 2/8 Marines began to get a bit moody. The majority of the troops of 2/8 were young, under age twenty-five, and as such, patience had not yet developed as a strong virtue in most of them. Even though they camped in Kuwait for only one month, attitudes developed in some of them. Some weren't convinced that action was imminent, and a rumor was circulating that Hussein's government was going to collapse. The company commanders worked to keep their men focused. "I would tell my guys, 'I'm certain 2/8 is going in,' whether it was for war or to provide security operations to help establish a new government," Capt. Yeo recalled.

In early March, Lt. Gen. Conway paid a visit to RCT-2 and 2/8. As the commanding officer of I MEF, which was made up of more than 60,000 Marines, Conway was visiting his units to encourage and embolden the men and women for the likely fight to come. Part of his speech focused on the technology advantages the U.S. forces would bring to bear in combat. He announced a new U.S. invention—"QuicKlot" bandages—that were being made available for the first time for combat. QuicKlots had been specifically developed for major bleeding wounds, thereby greatly increasing the chances of survival if the injured person was seriously wounded.

Mortenson took Gen. Conway's seminal announcement seriously. Upon Conway's exit, he made an immediate request to Col. Bailey to secure an allotment of the new bandages. Bailey's staff came through, and 2/8 received a good supply. This initiative by Mortenson would later prove to be life-saving in combat.

As war became imminent, David's prayers focused on asking God to protect 2/8, for good attitudes to prevail, and for God to cause fear to come upon the Iraqi military. In a letter home, dated March 7, David wrote: "Not everyone is given the opportunity to do what we are doing for our country....I'm so thankful to be part of this." He closed his letter with: "The Lord is consuming me with joy and happiness. May He do the same in your lives."

Back home, our family had been praying since the words spoken in church on February 9 that God would bring confusion and fear on the Iraqi forces and that He would give protection and wisdom to American and allied forces. In addition, God added another important prayer to our requests. He led us to ask Him to give David, his buddies, and the men of his company and battalion supernatural strength and endurance like the prophet Elijah received, as told in I Kings 18. After three and one-half years of drought in the land because of the Israelites' idolatry, Elijah won a showdown with false prophets on Mount Carmel, and then prayed for and received rain. The Spirit of God further came upon Elijah, and he outran evil King Ahab, who was riding to his summer palace in Jezreel, about seventeen miles away, to announce the outcome. A horse-drawn chariot like Ahab's could average fifteen miles per hour, or a four-minute-mile pace. Elijah outran this pace, and thus became the first human in recorded history to break the four-minute mile (sorry Roger Bannister), and he did it for seventeen miles!

Of course, this was a miraculous event, made possible only by the hand of God. The implication for David and the men of 2/8 was clear. They would need a supernatural boost of endurance from God to succeed in the manner God desired. This "Elijah" prayer became a daily request from our family and friends.

A very special and helpful answer to prayer occurred in 2/8 just a few days before the war began. The origins of the prayer could be traced back to December. At that time, during a meeting with the 2/8 family-support group—which consisted mostly of wives of battalion Marines—Mortenson had stated that if the battalion was deployed it would be difficult for families to receive news about their loved ones. This was primarily because no journalists were going to be "embedded," or assigned, to the battalion. After 2/8 received the order to deploy, several 2/8 wives—including Jen Alford, Catherine Dremann, and Andrea Yeo—began an organized prayer effort, asking God to provide a way for the families to receive news and to remove the barriers preventing regular communications from 2/8.

By mid-March, all embedded reporters had been approved by the Department of Defense (DOD) and assigned, leaving formal slots open only for roving reporters who would be confined well behind the forward lines of combat units. Kerry Sanders of NBC News had the necessary satellite communications equipment and staff to work as an embedded reporter with a forward unit but had not received such a favorable assignment. He and his team were facing the prospect of being stuck in the rear areas. Kerry approached Mortenson and asked if he could intervene and help NBC News and his team. Mortenson invited Kerry and his team to ride with 2/8 and managed to secure a seven-ton truck for their exclusive use. Those involved realized by the time the DOD approved a formal request that 2/8 would be halfway to Baghdad. So Mortenson made the decision on the spot to invite the NBC team to embed with his battalion. The prayers of the wives and families of 2/8 had been neatly answered. Kerry and his team would go on to provide daily reports and some of the best news coverage of the whole war.

The troops could sense the approach of war, and most took time to write a final letter to wives, husbands, and families back home before D-day came. Capt. Ross wrote an encouraging letter to his wife, Tracy, that discussed the difficult topic of being killed in combat and what the attitude toward the war should be if that happened. "If I don't come home, tell the boys I was just doing my job in serving my country," he wrote. "Don't harbor any ill feelings against anyone, and be proud of what we are doing and did over here. It *is* the right thing to do." It was as if Capt. Ross was speaking for the whole Marine Expeditionary Force. These Marines were motivated—heart, mind, and spirit. No shadow of turning, no equivocation would be found with the Marines of Operation Iraqi Freedom.

By the week of March 9 to March 16, Capt. Dupree was giving very specific intel briefs to the battalion in Kuwait, and later that week some ammunition was handed out. By Thursday, March 13, the battalion was packed up and ready to roll. In the United States on Monday night, March 17—which was early in the morning of the 18th in Kuwait—President Bush addressed the nation and world, giving Saddam Hussein forty-eight hours to leave Iraq with his sons or face war with America and its allied forces.

At that point it was perfectly clear to the men of 2/8 that war would come within hours. Mortenson noticed the differences in the faces of his men as the political reality sunk in. Any shades of boredom were gone. The Marines of 2/8 had their game faces on. The time to wage war was at hand.

4

LAUNCH

For You have armed me with strength for the battle.
—PSALM 18:39

Do not keep silent, O God! Do not hold Your peace, and do not be still, O God! For behold, Your enemies make a tumult; and those who hate You have lifted up their head.
—PSALM 83:1-2

First and foremost, Marines exist to fight and win.
—FROM *LEADING MARINES*

WHILE IN KUWAIT, GUNNY SWEENEY had been trying to help his men in Golf Company keep their minds free from worry and anticipation. "We're not going until they hand out the grenades," he often said. Wednesday, March 19, the grenades were handed out. The order was then given by Mortenson to have all 2/8 units assemble in formation and be ready to launch by 0700 the next day, March 20. From the late evening on the 19th and into the early morning of the 20th, 2/8 heard American fighter and attack planes flying overhead. Bombing could be heard in the distance. Operation Iraqi Freedom was underway.

In the United States, the start of the conflict brought an

immediate response for prayer to begin in earnest among believers. Christians across the country were unified with a great sense of urgency to pray. Capt. Yeo's wife, Andrea; her sister Patricia Williams of Farmington Hills, Michigan; his mother, Delores, in South Dakota and his five sisters were great examples of just one family's efforts. Delores "believes in prayer without ceasing," and with her church's prayer chain and her five daughters calling frequently, the prayers were constant for weeks to come. Andrea prayed every night, and over the course of the war she became the focal point in Echo Company for numerous prayers with the wives and families of her husband's Marines.

Andrea would come into direct contact through telephone conversations and e-mail with more than 50 families of the approximately 150 men in Echo Company. Parents and wives called or sent her e-mails. According to Andrea, "They were not shy about telling me, 'My church is praying for Kevin and Echo and 2/8.'" A Catholic by faith, Andrea found comfort as well in calling on her husband's guardian angel to protect him. Patricia Williams coordinated prayers within several Catholic groups. These included a prayer group of more than 20 believers at Trinity Health, her employer, which was led by Sister Catherine DeClerq, OP; a group of fifteen business associates at the Catholic Consortium for International Health Services; and the Religious Sisters of Mercy in Farmington Hills.

She and Andrea are natives of Argentina and still have many family members there, including two cousins who are Catholic priests. The sisters contacted their cousins, who reported back that they had coordinated prayers at several churches in Argentina. A conservative estimate of Christians praying in earnest for Echo Company and 2/8 was 2,000 believers from more than 50 churches—all through contacts made by Andrea and Patricia.

Capt. Ross's wife, Tracy, likewise was in contact with many wives and families within Golf Company. From the preparation days in January, when she posted prayers to recite on her refrigerator, her prayers with her own sons, her family, and other Marine families were frequent. Looking back on the time of combat, Tracy stated: "I never had a sense that Brian wouldn't come back, but there was a tension that was really only relieved in prayer. I don't know how you could make it through without prayer, without faith."

One of the most amazing stories of prayer that started with the onset of combat involved an organized effort that came into fruition largely because of Dr. Richard H. Pritchard, a retired U.S. Air Force Reserve Colonel and nuclear weapons expert. Pritchard had received an e-mail that told the story of an aide to Winston Churchill who, during the dark days of the Battle of Britain in World War II, organized a group of people to pray for England every night at 9:00. Moved by this example, Pritchard sent e-mails to every person in his address book, and those folks in turn sent it to their contacts. It quickly cascaded into thousands of people receiving Pritchard's original message. In that e-mail, after describing the World War II effort, Pritchard made a very simple request as follows: "If you would like to participate, every evening at 9 p.m. Eastern Time, stop whatever you are doing and spend one minute praying for the safety of the United States, its citizens, its men and women in the military, and for peace in the world."

The response to Pritchard's initiative was monumental. Over the next few weeks during the height of the war, he received fifty to one hundred e-mails a day from believers in the United States and around the world, from the United Kingdom, Australia, and other countries. Mothers, fathers, wives, brothers, and sisters of those serving, as well as veterans, including numerous Vietnam vets, all inundated him with e-mails and phone calls to say they were praying at 9 p.m. While interviewing Pritchard for this book, we quickly calculated that he received more than 1,000 e-mails alone, from which it can be reasonably estimated that 15,000 to 20,000 people or more probably were involved with this prayer effort. One of the habits of Jesus while He was in His earthly ministry was regular, consistent times of prayer. We may not know the specific details of God's answers to the massive number of repeated requests, but any person of faith would rec-ognize that the Lord must have loved and rewarded this type of dedication. Someday, we believe, we will fully know.

Back in Kuwait, as the units of 2/8 assembled in the early morning of the 20th, CAAT platoon commander Capt. Seth

MacCutcheon walked up to Chaplain Rogers and asked, "Hey, Chaplain, before we leave would you mind praying over my vehicles?" MacCutcheon commanded the four CAAT sections, named Black, Green, Gold, and Scarlet. Each section had four Humvees equipped with TOW anti-tank missiles, MK-19 grenade launchers, .50-caliber machine guns, and a Javelin anti-tank missile team. Their job was to find and destroy enemy armor before the enemy could attack the bulk of the battalion.

Chaplain Rogers understood the seriousness of MacCutcheon's request. "CAAT teams are the furthest ones out—whoever is going to get fired upon first, nine times out of ten it's going to be them," Rogers said later. "When Seth asked me to pray, I knew we had some time—we weren't going to leave in twenty minutes—so I prayed over his vehicles. Then I laid hands on every vehicle in 2/8—over seventy Humvees and trucks, praying that the vehicle would not be hit and for the safety of the men who would ride in them. I prayed about twenty seconds over each one," Rogers described. Rogers' efforts did not go unnoticed. Unknown to the chaplain, Maj. Fulford caught a glimpse of Rogers methodically praying and moving from vehicle to vehicle. "It was one of the highlights I will always remember," Fulford said later. "I vividly remember him doing this."

Around 0800, Mortenson called all of his Marines together. He spoke with elegant simplicity. "There is no finer battalion, no battalion more prepared to do this," he said. "We have a destiny, and the way home for us is north, through Baghdad!" Sgt. Maj. Thorne spoke next. With characteristic bluntness, he urged his Marines onward. "We've been waiting for this chance to stick our bayonets into someone!" he said. Chaplain Rogers then prayed for the battalion, in front of the men, asking for God's protection, courage, and single-mindedness of purpose. "I always wanted to remind the guys there is a God out there," he said.

The battalion departed around 1300 local time and moved up to Tactical Assembly Area (TAA) Hawkins, only a couple of miles from the Iraqi border, and spent the night there. They were now well within range of Iraqi missiles and artillery. The war was being waged overhead from where they stood. "We saw lots of

MLRS rockets flying overhead toward Iraq," David recalled. "And we saw Patriot missiles going off, shooting down SCUDS. It was like a fireworks show." The MLRS is a powerful long range tactical rocket typically launched in large numbers by U.S. Army and Marine units for massive bombardment of enemy positions. Mortenson also described that night's aerial engagements. "It was a great light show," he said, adding, "We definitely saw Patriots intercepting incoming SCUDS."

It may never be known whether the Iraqis were targeting 2/8 or other Marine and Army positions near the border, but they for sure were firing into Kuwait. Unlike the Persian Gulf War, when Patriot missiles missed more incoming SCUDS than they hit, this time the improved Patriots were spectacular. Only one or two Iraqi missiles got by that night, and they landed harmlessly in the desert. It would turn out that throughout Operation Iraqi Freedom no American forces became casualties from Iraqi missiles. The answers to millions of prayers for the protection of U.S. and allied forces had begun, and RCT-2 and 2/8 were among the first who benefited.

On the morning of Friday, March 21, 2/8 crossed into Iraq. "We were excited," David recalled. "We all wanted to shoot." Their time to see action would have to wait, however, for another two days. Throughout the 21st and 22nd, 2/8 encountered no resistance. "Two days of nothing," David said. "We were wondering when we would see action." Capt. Ross described these days. "[There were] a lot of boring convoy movements. Each night we'd stop and prepare defensive positions. I'd walk around and talk to my Marines. By the night of the 22nd we had driven over one hundred miles into Iraq and hadn't seen any Iraqi soldiers, just a few Bedouin. On the night of the 22nd I told my guys, 'This country is the size of California—we're going to come across somebody!'"

It wasn't as if they were isolated from the action. Throughout these first two days they could hear planes, bombing, and artillery fire—and they could feel the ground shaking. Each night to the west they could see convoys of the Army's Third Mechanized Infantry Division (3rd ID) in the distance with their lights on. "It looked like an interstate...loads of tanks, armored vehicles, refuelers, water trucks, Humvees," Ross said. David remembers thinking, *I'm glad we don't have to fight those guys.*

As 2/8 rolled north, tension and alertness increased among the men. "After a couple of days in Iraq this stabilized and stayed at a high awareness level," Capt. Yeo would recall. "You have confidence you're going to win; you don't have confidence about how much it's going to cost. I know there is no nation who can stand toe-to-toe with the U.S. What it would cost a rifle company was really the question."

The standard command structure for an infantry battalion in war separates the battalion CO and XO into two command posts. The senior staff goes with the battalion CO, and the bulk of H&S Company is located with the XO. Mortenson, Fulford, Dupree, Luciano, and communications and security Marines occupied TAC CP (or TAC), for "tactical command post." TAC was kept very lean—intentionally, to increase its mobility and to make it hard for the enemy to locate it. The TAC security unit consisted of Marines manning 4 Humvees with mounted MK-19, .50-caliber and M240 Golf machine guns. Alford—with the assistant S2 and assistant S3s, the bulk of H&S service units, and the log train—were located in the Main CP, or main command post—Main for short.

TAC and Main do much the same job. One is active and the other is on standby, listening in. This not only ensures 24/7 command coverage, but it also helps to keep the battalion fully functional should one of the posts be hit.

The relatively slow buildup to combat was probably good for the men of 2/8, as well as for the civilian reporters who had been embedded with the battalion. Kerry Sanders and his crew had begun filing reports on the progress of 2/8 with NBC-TV. Having Kerry embedded with the battalion would draw a mixed response from families back home over the course of the conflict. Many people—including John Cain's parents and sisters; Capt. Yeo's wife, Andrea, and his sister-in-law Patricia Williams; Capt. Dremann's wife, Catherine; and I—found the TV reports to be a big help. At times we would be glued to the news. For us, Kerry's daily reports were both informative and very useful for helping direct our family's daily prayers. It was also a great comfort to know exactly where the battalion was.

But there were some family members, such as 1st Lt. Chad Ragan's wife, Becky, and my wife, Pam, who found the TV reports too intense for their liking. Lt. Ragan was at this time the assistant S3 operations officer, located with Maj. Alford in the Main CP. However within the battalion, the Marines were most often thankful that their families and loved ones back home would be kept well-informed of 2/8's progress.

In addition to Kerry and his team, a French free-lance photographer, Eric Feferberg, was allowed to ride with Golf Company. Ross assigned him to Second Platoon, and he rode in the same truck as David's First Squad. These first couple of slow days allowed First Squad ample opportunity to harass Feferberg. "We'd pile in the truck, and he'd typically be the last one in" David said. "He would whine, 'I have no room to sit,' and we'd just yell, 'Sit down and shut up!' He really had as much room as we did; he just liked to complain." Sgt. Campbell couldn't resist needling him. "How come you French haven't won a war in like the last millennium?" he'd ask Feferberg, who couldn't come up with much of an answer.

Until the night of the 22nd, the Iraqi resistance had been completely ineffective. On the afternoon of March 21, back in Washington and at about 9 p.m. in Iraq, Secretary of Defense Donald Rumsfeld stated in a press conference: "The confusion of the Iraqi leadership is growing." This was the first reported confirmation to specific prayers that God had led His people to pray, and it emboldened many believers back home, including our family, to continue to be steadfast in prayer.

Later in the day of March 22, as 2/8 approached An-Nasiriyah, the men could feel and hear the sounds of heavy artillery rounds as well as bombs and rockets launched from U.S. combat aircraft landing on targets in and around the city. Everyone now knew that the time for 2/8 to become engaged in combat was fast approaching. The command message from Mortenson passed on to every troop was simple. Stay on your toes. Don't get complacent. Be patient and be ready for when it comes.

The plans for Task Force Tarawa called for the ground element

RCT-2 supported by Marine Air Group 29 to move up Highway 8 and onto Highway 7 to capture two key bridges in An-Nasiriyah. The southern bridge spanned the Euphrates River, and the northern bridge the Saddam Canal. Controlling this route and the bridges was essential for enabling other ground-combat units and supplies to continue to move north, especially for I MEF. Without continual, fresh provisions from the rear supply units of the large amounts of fuel, ammunition, water and food consumed in combat, the advance of ground units would screech to a halt within a day or two. Stagnant ground forces are easier targets than maneuvering forces for enemy attacks, and typically lead to higher casualty rates. Gaining control of the two bridges was absolutely paramount to the success of I MEF and the U.S. battle plan.

Colonel Bailey had already decided that Lt. Col. Grabowski's First Battalion-Second Marines would be the lead unit into An-Nasiriyah and would push north over the Euphrates River bridge to capture the bridge over the Saddam Canal. Bailey's selection of 1/2 as the lead unit was based partly on the fact that the battalion contained the main armored elements from his regiment. Both 2/8 and Lt. Col. Dunahoe's 3/2 would follow 1/2 into the city. One battalion would be assigned part of the main objective to seize and control Highway 7 up to and including the southern Euphrates River bridge. The remaining battalion would sweep west in a supporting role to control the left flank of RCT-2's positions.

Bailey had planned before RCT-2 left Kuwait to have 2/8 push up behind 1/2 into the city, using 3/2 to control the western flank. Bailey later explained the factors that influenced his plans. "Royal had been in command longer than any of my other commanders—other than Glenn Starnes, the artillery commander," he said. "I also knew they had just come out of Bridgeport; the year before they'd been in CAX. As I was walking around meeting these guys, I noticed they had this unusual amount of chemistry. I could tell they were very tight. I instantly hit it off with [Mortenson], the XO, the staff, the sergeant major, and the company commanders. I could just sense it. I felt I had to make a decision to make sure that 2/8 knew that I believed in them and that they felt they were part of the team."

The assignment for 3/2 had more unknowns, perhaps, regarding the strength of the enemy than the assignments for 1/2 and 2/8. Bailey accordingly attached some heavy hitting units to 3/2. "We gave 3/2 the LAR Company because I needed them to have something to defend themselves with if they hit more out west than I could envision," he recalled later. Although Bailey had planned the roles for 2/8 and 3/2 before leaving Kuwait, he hadn't cast their assignments in stone, and he had time to change his plan if desired. The tentative orders for RCT-2 to move into the city were set by the night of the 22nd.

An-Nasiriyah is a city of approximately 300,000 people and thus the likelihood of urban warfare and its typically high casualty rates loomed large. Bailey, his BCs and their senior staffs all knew that if the Iraqis decided to fight in the city, it could become a difficult battle. Early in the morning of March 23, Bailey and RCT-2 received orders to execute the seizure of the two bridges. In just a few hours, Task Force Tarawa and 2/8 would become fully engaged in their first, and what would prove to be their toughest, day of combat in the war.

5

An-Nasiriyah:
March 23 to March 24

And under His wings you shall take refuge; His truth shall be your shield and buckler. You shall not be afraid of the terror by night, nor of the arrow that flies by day, nor of the pestilence that walks in darkness, nor of the destruction that lays waste at noonday.

—Psalm 91:4-6

Success in battle is not a function of how many show up, but who they are.

—Gen. Robert H. Barrow, USMC,
from *Leading Marines*

A unit led by an able and aggressive leader who commands respect because he set the example and demonstrated courage and confidence will perform any task asked of them.

—Charles Edmundson, "Why Warriors Fight,"
from *Leading Marines*

As dawn came on Sunday, March 23, Task Force Tarawa began their move into An-Nasiriyah. An-Nasiriyah was the headquarters for the Iraqi Eleventh Infantry Division, and U.S. intelligence was uncertain about the Eleventh Division's loyalty to Hussein's regime. Apparently Hussein was concerned about their loyalty, as well, because he assigned large numbers of Fedayeen militiamen to the city to help ensure that the Eleventh Division would stay and fight. The Fedayeen were fanatical Iraqi militiamen sworn to defend Hussein. What they lacked in formal infantry training they compensated for somewhat with their passion and dedication. They disregarded the rules of the Geneva Convention by dressing and fighting in civilian clothing, and, as shall be shown in this book, they typically employed tactics the Marines considered despicable, cowardly, and in further violation of the Geneva Convention.

First in for Task Force Tarawa was First Battalion-Second Marines. The conceptual plan for 1/2 called for Alpha Company to seize and hold the southern Euphrates River bridge. This would allow Bravo and Charlie Companies with attached tank units to cross the Euphrates bridge and move north to secure the bridge.

Approximately 4,000 meters separate the two bridges, which are connected by a straight slab of Highway 7 running north-south. Lt. Col. Grabowski never intended to send Bravo and Charlie Companies up the obvious shortest distance to the Canal bridge, along Highway 7. Instead, he planned to have Bravo Company cross the Euphrates, loop east and establish a support by fire position to the east of Highway 7, to enable him to bring fire to bear down onto the Saddam Canal bridge area if necessary.

The Canal bridge was prime real estate, and it was reasonable to assume that if the Iraqis were going to fight, it would be in large part to defend the northern bridge, and thus a strong support by fire position would need to be established by 1/2. Once Bravo Company was established east of Highway 7, Grabowski intended to send Charlie Company over the Euphrates bridge and loop east and behind Bravo, then advance north and seize the canal bridge with an attack from the east supported by Bravo Company. With anticipated Iraqi resistance along Highway 7 between the two bridges, Grabowski planned to sweep east of these positions with this flanking move and seize the bridge from the east.

The attack of 1/2 ran into an unexpected situation early on. As Alpha Company advanced along Highway 7 toward the Euphrates River bridge, they ran into the destroyed vehicles of the U.S. Army's 507th Maintenance Company—the unit of Jessica Lynch, Lori Piestawa, Shoshanna Johnson, and other now well-known young soldiers. The 507th had been ambushed shortly before Alpha arrived. Alpha Company stopped to deal with the 507th situation and ran into Iraqi resistance, and thus had to fight its way to the Euphrates bridge. This caused some delay in the timing of 1/2's attack plan, and required Alpha Company to expend more fuel and ammunition than expected. However, Alpha Company advanced and seized the Euphrates bridge by mid-morning.

Bravo Company then advanced to Alpha Company's position, crossed the Euphrates bridge, and swept to the east of Highway 7 as planned. The eastern terrain quickly turned very muddy, and the company vehicles and tanks attached to Bravo began to get bogged down. The ground conditions worsened, into almost swamplike conditions, and Bravo's Humvees, tracked vehicles and tanks started to become stuck in the muddy areas. Due largely to the delay caused by the ground conditions, the Iraqis were able to locate Bravo's position, reposition themselves and fire on Bravo with mortars, machine guns, and small arms. Bravo Company was now embroiled in a full-fledged firefight. The whole Bravo Company attack bogged down as they both fought the Iraqis and worked to move their vehicles out of the mud.

The situation for 1/2 was difficult but workable at this time, with Bravo in a major firefight and now Alpha Company in a fight to hold the Euphrates River bridge. But then disaster struck. Grabowski's TAC CP command element was also located with Bravo Company, and the antenna from the battalion's main high-power radio hit a low lying overhead utility power line, which damaged Grabowski's main radio and caused 1/2 to lose their encrypted communications. With the loss of primary communications, Grabowski had no ability to effectively command and control his battalion, especially the maneuver elements of 1/2. The only operable radios were the lower-powered units with whip antennas mounted on the backs of Marine radiomen in each company. These radios typically require stationary line-of-sight clearance to receive and transmit, and during fighting the whip antennas are moving around with their host Marines, making communications spotty at best.

Charlie Company moved up to Alpha Company, crossed the Euphrates bridge and began to head straight down Highway 7 toward the canal bridge. Grabowski was unable to get orders to Charlie Company to loop east as planned. Thinking Bravo Company had already pushed through and was in a supporting position, Charlie continued down Highway 7 for the 4,000 meters and came under fire the whole way. Amazingly, Charlie Company made it to the Saddam Canal with very few casualties and seized the bridge.

Events then took a bloody turn for Charlie Company. Elements of the company pushed north over the Canal bridge and found themselves at the focal point of a large amount of Iraqi fire. A major fight began over the north side of the bridge. Charlie Company began receiving hits from RPGs, small-arms fire, heavy machine-gun fire, and indirect artillery rounds. The company began taking more casualties. The 60 mm mortar section of Charlie took a direct hit from an Iraqi mortar or artillery round, causing several casualties. Wounded Marines were loaded into five tracked vehicles to be evacuated south to the regimental field hospital, and they headed back down Highway 7.

This time, all five tracked vehicles took hits fired from the buildings and behind trees lining the highway. One vehicle was disabled and drove off the road, and the Marines onboard dismounted and dashed into a nearby house and began to fight determinedly from there, isolated from the rest of the battalion. The remaining four vehicles made it to the Euphrates bridge and linked up with Alpha Company. One of these four suddenly took several hits from RPGs while at the bridge, killing the wounded Marines inside the vehicle. The remaining three vehicles then managed to make it south from the Euphrates bridge to Mortenson's TAC and 2/8's battalion aid station, where 2/8 Marines began unloading and treating the wounded. The stretch of Highway 7 between the Euphrates and Canal bridges was quickly dubbed "ambush alley."

But the tribulation for Charlie Company of 1/2 was not over yet. To support the 1/2 attack to seize the canal bridge, close air-support missions were cleared to attack north of the canal bridge. The fearsome U.S. Air Force A-10 attack jets with their deadly armor-busting Gatling-style guns were tasked to fill the request. Unaware, because of the communications failure, that Charlie Company was already positioned at and fighting over the canal bridge, the A-10s rolled in on the fight thinking that anything north of the canal bridge was the enemy. In their

OVERVIEW OF RCT-2 POSITIONS
BATTLE FOR AN-NASIRIYAH

MARCH 23–APRIL 3, 2003

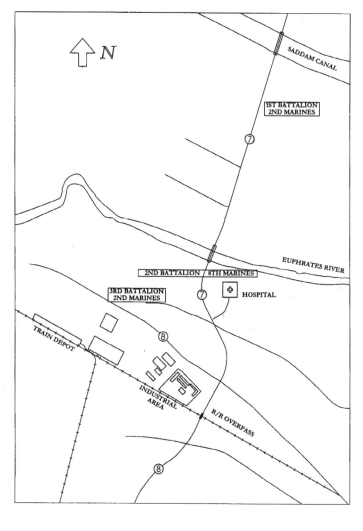

attack they accidentally struck two armored vehicles from Charlie Company, killing nine more Marines. The total killed in 1/2 throughout the day's fight was eighteen men. Dozens more were wounded.

From their TAC just outside of An-Nasiriyah, Mortenson and his Marines were dealing with the evacuated dead and wounded of 1/2 when Bailey called and ordered Mortenson and 2/8 into the city. Bailey later recalled, "This was probably the most important decision I made during the execution of the combat. It was at that moment that we thrust 2/8 into the fight."

Mortenson was more than ready to get into the battle. He called his company commanders up to TAC to quickly finalize their plans for entering the city. It was then that Mortenson made what he would later call the key decision of the whole war for 2/8. "I flat out made the decision there would be no-holds-barred," he said. "We weren't going to risk Marines' lives. We weren't going to hesitate. The Iraqi forces made their decision to fight, and we were going to finish it."

As his company commanders assembled, he drove his point home, underscoring that 1/2 was in a heavy fight in An-Nasiriyah and telling his officers how 2/8 would reinforce 1/2. "From now on," he told them, "if someone shoots at my Marines with an AK-47 from a second-story window, I'll take out the whole [expletive] second floor! If they shoot at us with a mortar, we're going to shoot back with artillery."

The officers very quickly came up with a battle plan and fine-tuned it on the spot. "I remember talking with my Golf Platoon commanders as to the plan with the radio in one hand, and then Major Fulford getting on the radio and changing it," Ross said. The plan called for Dremann's Fox company to lead in and secure the southern bridge, Yeo's Echo company would follow and sweep and clear the west side of Highway 7, and Ross's Golf Company would pull behind Echo and clear and hold the east side of the highway.

A key element of the plan called for Fox Company to link up with Alpha Company from 1/2 and relieve them at the Euphrates bridge, to allow 1/2 to consolidate their positions north of the bridge. In addition, at some point 1/2 would need to be reprovisioned from their log train, as 1/2 was beginning to run low on fuel and ammunition from their engagement. Their log train was still south of the city, and Mortenson wanted to make sure he provided a secure route to allow 1/2 to reload.

On the outskirts south of the city on Highway 8, the men of 2/8 saw Marine Cobra attack helicopters flying overhead and could hear missiles exploding and see smoke plumes rising in the distance. Their vehicle convoys passed burning Iraqi tanks. They all knew the regiment was now engaged. Elements of Mac-Cutcheon's CAAT platoon formed the lead unit from 2/8 heading into An-Nasiriyah with Dremman's men in trucks following close behind. At that time, Dremann assumed 1/2 had cleared Highway 7. The CAAT elements and Fox Company had passed north of the grid-point coordinate where they were supposed to link up with 1/2, but Alpha Company had already moved north to reinforce Charlie Company in their fight.

Immediately, the CAAT vehicles and Fox Company started taking heavy machine-gun fire from the west side of Highway 7. It was now obvious the area had not been cleared, and Dremann ordered Fox and MacCutcheon to pull back to a covered dismount position. It was a very tense few minutes as the men dismounted from their trucks under fire and pulled back a short distance south to Phase Line Jackie to start clearing the area. "We were extremely vulnerable at that time. I don't think you can contribute Fox not taking a RPG round or something else in there to much other than divine intervention," Dremann would recall. "Had we taken a big hit we would have had a lot of men killed." This is the first of what would become many miracles of protection for 2/8 while under direct enemy fire.

Fox Company began to clear houses on the west side of Highway 7, and Dremann began talking to Maj. Fulford over the radio. "Do we systematically clear this road, or do we need to get to the bridge as quickly as possible?" Dremann asked Fulford. "We need you to get to the bridge as quick as you can," Fulford replied. They both knew a careful, methodical clearing of every house and building along the road to the bridge would take three to four hours. Fulford couldn't afford the time.

After completing their discussion, Dremann reloaded his Marines into their vehicles and drove Fox Company straight through to the Euphrates bridge. Not a single shot was fired at them as they advanced along the highway. Fully expecting to have to fight his way to the bridge, Dremann was pleasantly surprised. "It was amazing," he recalled. Apparently the Iraqis had abandoned most or all of their positions along this southern stretch of Highway 7, including the areas around the site of the 507th's ambush and northward to the Euphrates bridge, the same areas that 1/2's Alpha Company had fought through just hours before. After seeing the 1/2 Marines moving north over the Euphrates bridge, the Iraqis had likely moved their soldiers and Fedayeen north to consolidate their strength in their fight with 1/2. Reaching the bridge, Dremann placed one of his rifle platoons west and one east of the south side of the bridge, with the third platoon positioned on the bridge. A key component of 2/8's battle plan had been fulfilled.

Next up was Yeo with Echo Company. He didn't waste any time. His men quickly and methodically swept up and cleared the west side of Highway 7, wiping out some pockets of Iraqi resistance that were trying to move back into concealed attack positions along the highway. Certainly the Iraqis could now see that Fox Company had taken control of the southern bridge, and they realized that their exit to the north was premature. What they didn't count on was Yeo's Marines following close behind, and Echo caught them off guard.

In relatively short order, the lead elements of Echo Company met Fox Company at the bridge, while the rest of Echo secured the west side of the road. This allowed Dremann to redeploy his west-positioned rifle platoon to strengthen his eastern flank. The defensive perimeter around the bridge was now rock solid, and 2/8 had taken no casualties in the process.

As Echo Company advanced, Golf Company began its move north. Their initial orders had been finalized to clear the southwest side of Highway 7 where the Fedayeen had fired on Fox Company and then to clear and hold the east side of the highway.

Ross had concerns that Golf would possibly be heading into an ambush like 1/2 had seen, but the tension was broken by a bit of comic relief. As his truck headed toward the city, his driver turned to him and said, "Good luck to y'all, sir. I hope y'all do well." Ross shot back, "You're driving to the same place I am!"—after which the driver remained silent.

While Golf rode toward the city line, David got a warm feeling from seeing Cobra attack choppers overhead and hearing 1/10 artillery hitting targets to the north. "We were locked and loaded," he said. Soon after entering An-Nasiriyah—around 2 p.m.—Golf began receiving small-arms fire from AK-47s and 74s. *This is the real deal*, David thought.

Ross immediately ordered his troops out of the vehicles. Their training began to take over. The sergeants took his orders and got their Marines moving. The platoons and squads quickly went about their business. The fire teams began to fan out, looking for the Iraqi firing positions. It wasn't long before Golf's sniper teams began opening up with counterfire. David's First Squad-Second Platoon cleared some houses, then advanced north and cleared a school.

Several images stuck in David's mind during this initial taste of combat that would be seen and reinforced over and over again throughout the war. The first was the artwork of school children, drawn undoubtedly under instruction from teachers and unmistakable in content. It was pictures of the World Trade Center towers on fire, with planes drawn crashing into them. *These nuts are teaching these kids that murder is good*, David thought, and it made him angry. The drawings also fired up every other Marine who saw and heard about them, which was bad news for the Iraqi soldiers. Other warped artwork included drawings of the American flag being trampled by Iraqi soldiers and tanks, Elvis Presley with his throat slit, and President Bush and U.S. Army generals being set on fire. A second set of images was that of Iraqi civilians walking on Highway 7, seemingly indifferent to the automatic-weapons fire and gunfire exchanges. David quickly began questioning in his mind their lackadaisical attitudes. He wondered if any were complicit with those shooting at them.

While Golf Company advanced, farther north Fox was receiving heavy machine-gun fire from the north side of the bridge. Rounds were whipping by the unit's positions, and the machine guns were hidden well enough to prevent Fox from easily destroying them. A few Iraqi mortar rounds began to land near them, but no casualties were taken.

These days enemy mortar and artillery personnel are virtually on a suicide mission thanks to counter-battery radar used by the Marines and the U.S. Army in combat. This radar has the speed and resolution to detect not only incoming mortar and artillery rounds, but also their trajectories, which gives American commanders the precise location of the enemy. If the enemy fires more than one or two rounds without relocating his position, then he is very likely sealing his fate. Firing even one round is risky when counter-battery radar is operating.

After the first few Iraqi mortar rounds hit, Fox Company's forward observer called TAC for fire support, and Mortenson chose to fire back with 81 mm mortars from Luciano's Weapons Company. Luciano checked the coordinates and approved the fire mission, and the mortar rounds landed on target, destroying the Iraqi mortars. Apparently, Weapons Company's mortars also took out the Iraqi machine gun placements because they stopped shooting as well.

Throughout the day as the Marines of Fox, Echo, and Golf fought their way north, they moved past the burning U.S. Army vehicles from the 507th Maintenance Company that sat in the middle of Highway 7. The vehicles were situated north of east-west Highway 8 but south of the southern bridge across the Euphrates. It was obvious that several American soldiers had died there. Blood stains marked the doors of the vehicles. What 2/8 did not know at this time was that several American soldiers had been captured, including female soldiers Lynch, Piestawa, and Johnson.

Later on the afternoon of March 23, 2/8 started receiving intelligence about these missing soldiers. Fox Company had taken twelve Iraqi enemy prisoners of war (EPWs), and Capt. Dupree's human exploitation team (HET) had begun interrogations. One EPW told Dupree's team that two female American POWs were being held in the eastern hospital in An-Nasiriyah. This hospital was close, about 300 meters east of Dremann's defensive perimeter for the bridge and 500 meters or so northeast of Golf's perimeter. Dupree took note. "This single source report wasn't gospel, but it was information we could act on," he said later. "I went to Lt. Col. Mortenson and told him, 'We have a pretty good indication that American POWs are in that hospital.'"

The TAC had heard of the ambush, but they didn't know the extent of the action. This Iraqi EPW's information started weighing on Dupree. "It was the first time we realized there were American POWs, and they were close," he said. Dupree requested and received a list from the Army of twelve soldiers missing in action. Because the list contained only first name initials with last names, he couldn't determine which ones were women.

OVERVIEW 2/8 POSITIONS
BATTLE FOR AN-NASIRIYAH

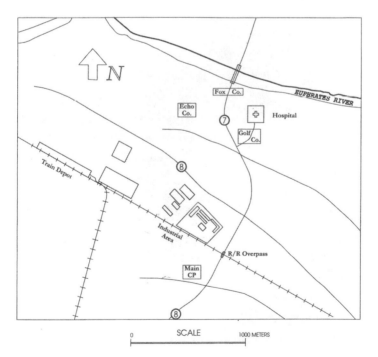

Dupree started praying, asking the Lord not to let him take counsel from his fears, and praying for inner strength. He then prayed, "Lord, if there are two American POWs in this hospital, please give us the time to allow us to go get them out of there." Dupree conferred with Mortenson, and they agreed that at some point the Iraqis would probably move the POWs. Mortenson, however, had a hunch that if they were injured, then they were likely to still be in the eastern hospital. Mortenson needed more information, though, before he could decide whether to attempt a rescue mission at the hospital.

As the first day in An-Nasiriyah turned into late afternoon, Golf completed its clearing operations and secured the east side of Highway 7. All three rifle companies had set up defensive positions, and the Marines dug fighting holes to spend the night. Nobody would sleep this night. "Everyone was wide awake," David said. The first day of combat had been a resounding success for 2/8. Every objective had been met. Amazingly, there were no casualties. And the miracles of protection and favor were just beginning. For Fulford, it was the first day of a five-day sequence that he would never forget. "It was a surreal first day," he noted.

A lot had happened. With Highway 7 and the southern bridge firmly under control of the battalion, the Iraqis now would have to come out to fight to unseat 2/8 from its strategic positions. Every 2/8 Marine knew the battle for An-Nasiriyah was far from over.

Back home in western New York at around 9:30 p.m. Eastern Time, or 5:30 a.m. of Monday, March 24, in Iraq, our family had just watched NBC-TV's Sanders' report that Echo and Fox companies had secured the southern bridge in An-Nasiriyah. Seeing his report was both exciting and comforting.

We had a full house as we gathered to pray. In addition to Pam and me—and David's sisters Kelly, Becky, and Sarah, and his brother Nathan—there were friends of the kids that included Erin Hawkins and Andy Lyons. Erin led off with a strong conviction that God wanted us to pray for the feet of David and the other 2/8 Marines, asking God to keep them healthy and free from infections. This was such an important need now that 2/8 was in combat that we added it to our daily list of prayers. Andy asked God to somehow allow David to be comforted by seeing us praying as a family for him. Just a few minutes later Becky became very excited. "I can see David!" she cried out. She was experiencing a brief vision. "He's sitting there on a sand bank, looking up with a big smile on his face!" she exclaimed.

We weren't sure if David was sitting on a sand bank having a similar vision of us, as Andy had prayed, but upon his return after the war David confirmed that what Becky had seen actually happened. "There were many times when I had brief images, visions of you all praying," he said. "I could even hear the prayers at times. And I thank God, it helped me a lot." We continued to pray at that time for God to give 2/8 and allied forces His three-fold protection as well as Elijah-like supernatural endurance, wisdom, and discernment, to replace all fear with courage, and for confusion and fear to be upon the Iraqi military. For our family, God's manifestation through prayer encouraged us to keep at it.

Early the next morning, around 5:30 a.m. Eastern Time, I spent some quiet time before the Lord and again prayed for David. The Holy Spirit gave me a brief vision. I'm not given to seeing things, so this was a special event for me. I saw David standing with his combat gear, and a transparent, bell-shaped shield was all around him, covering him completely. The shield was very thick, uniformly about one foot thick all around. I had a warm sense in my heart and knew immediately what the Holy Spirit was showing me: that God was divinely protecting David, and nothing was going to get through that shielding.

In An-Nasiriyah, during the night of the 23rd and into the early morning of the 24th, the TAC CP and Main CP kept busy. Mortenson was concerned about his staff exhausting themselves in a protracted conflict, so he ordered his men to make use of downtime. "You will not burn yourselves out. You're no good to the battalion if you do," he told his staff.

Fulford used his downtime to reflect and pray, and his prayers had taken on a different focus since 2/8 had gone into combat. He now had a day-to-day focus. "Lord, help us survive this day"; "Lord, give us wisdom for the decisions that we need to make today," he would pray. Dupree likewise used his downtime to pray and reflect. Mortenson would later state, "We had plenty of time to think about decisions. Whether you went to the Lord or simply asked for guidance, you reflect." Upon further reflection after the combat was over, Mortenson became firmly convinced that the effects of everyone's prayers helped him to focus and avoid distractions. "I definitely felt a sense of focus," he said.

Early in the morning of Tuesday, March 24, a supply convoy was formed from the support vehicles of 1/2's log train. The orders were to move across the Euphrates River bridge and reprovision Charlie and Alpha companies at the canal bridge. The only viable route after crossing the Euphrates bridge was to run right up ambush alley. But Bailey, Grabowski, and Mortenson weren't about to allow the convoy to "run the gauntlet" and give the Iraqis a clear shot at them without first blasting enemy positions. It was decided that the 81 mm mortars in 2/8's Weapons Company were in the best position to provide support by fire, and Mortenson called on Luciano to coordinate the attack.

Luciano knew what it was like to fire a series in controlled exercises, but this was now real, unrestrained combat. He had taken the time in advance to lay out the whole city with on-call targets to be fired upon quickly when requested. He had even handed out grid-coordinate cards to the various companies and platoons. But this would be the first fire mission he had been totally responsible for.

The plan called for landing 81 mm mortar rounds on each side of Highway 7 in alternating fashion, in a zigzag pattern, and to progress the fire north heading up to 1/2's positions by the canal bridge. The convoy would follow close behind the detonating progression of mortar rounds. It was a bold plan, and required precise timing and very accurate placement. Luciano had two major concerns, collateral damage and friendly fire casualties, and he wanted none of either. "I did some intense praying," Luciano said later. "I prayed, 'Lord, allow this series to work!'"

The fire was devastating, and the supply convoy made it through ambush alley unscathed. Luciano's prayer had been answered, and then some. No friendly fire casualties were taken, and the 81s from 2/8 had convinced any Iraqi soldiers and

Fedayeen who survived to either abandon their positions or stay covered long enough for the convoy to pass safely.

A little later in the morning of the 24th, two Iraqi men—one an interpreter and the other a father with his two children—walked up to Second Platoon of Golf Company and stated, "We know where there are two American male POWs and two American female POWs in the hospital just north of here." After a brief discussion, Capt. Ross formed a patrol with Sgt. Campbell's First Squad-Second Platoon, which had just gotten back from clearing some farmhouses near their positions. Ross joined the patrol along with 1st Sgt. Beith, Pfc. Matt Mengel—the radio operator for Second Platoon—and some machine-gunners from Weapons Platoon, about eighteen men total. "We're going to knock on the hatch of the hospital," Ross told Campbell.

Taking the four Iraqis with them, they headed north toward the bridge, where they met up with an infantry platoon from Fox Company. A little excitement came as an RPG round hit the bridge, and a mortar round landed within 50 meters of them. *This is where the heat's on*, Ross thought. David wasn't sure of the "friendly" Iraqis' intention. "It did seem fishy that this Iraqi man with his kids would risk himself. If seen, the Iraqi military would kill him," David recalled later. Fortunately, there was a ledge in the terrain that allowed the patrol, the Fox platoon, and the four Iraqis to advance toward the hospital undetected. "The hospital was flying the Red Crescent [akin to a Red Cross flag], but also had sandbags all around," Ross said. "The hospital didn't look like a hospital," David would recall. "It had bunkers and Iraqi Army trucks around it."

Ross convinced one of the Iraqi men to go to the hospital, look around, and come back. After about an hour the Iraqi returned, claiming, "There are no Americans in there." Ross then sent Campbell's squad toward the hospital, and they lined up under a berm in tactical formation, all motivated to go in. Campbell requested permission from Ross to clear the hospital. Ross thought the better of it. He called Campbell's squad back. "We had only eighteen Marines," he said later. "The job really needed at least a whole company, given the likely number of Iraqi soldiers in the place."

Ross and his men headed back to Golf's main position while the Fox platoon remained close to the hospital.

Back at the TAC, the reports of American POWs provided earlier in the day by Golf Company, coupled with the Iraqi EPW reports the previous evening, were enough for Mortenson and Fulford to decide the hospital required some attention. In the early afternoon, Fulford called Ross to come down to the TAC, which was located about 1,000 meters south of Golf's position. "You need to do a cordon and search of the hospital," Fulford told Ross, and he assigned two sections from MacCutcheon's CAAT platoon as an attachment to assist Golf.

About the time Ross left to return to Golf, Mortenson left the TAC with his Humvee and some security Marines and drove north to meet up with Fox Company at the Euphrates bridge. Elements of the Second Light Armored Reconnaissance Battalion were crossing the bridge and heading north to support 1/2. Several senior officers from I MEF and Task Force Tarawa were at the Euphrates bridge observing, including Lt. Gen. Conway; Col. Johnson, the Task Force Tarawa G3 (operations staff officer); and Col. Bailey.

It was 2:30 p.m. in Iraq and 6:30 a.m. in western New York. Right about that time I was in morning prayers for 2/8. There was an unusual intensity this morning as I called upon God to place His hedge around David, his buddies, Golf Company, and 2/8 for the whole day. I was led to ask God to place His unction upon those in combat so they would call upon the Lord themselves. Unknown to those family and friends praying at home or to the Marines in An-Nasiriyah, 2/8 would in just a few minutes need every ounce of protection God was willing to provide.

As he returned to Golf, Ross briefed his platoon commanders and then ordered the company to form on-line in a staggered tactical column along an east-west dirt road that joined into Highway 7. The column stretched about 450 meters, with Third Platoon about 50 meters west of the small village cleared earlier in the day and with the CAAT sections and Second Platoon in the lead closest to Highway 7, about 500 meters west of the village. Weapons platoon and First Platoon were situated in between

First and Third platoons. It was about 3 p.m. Iraqi time.

Just as the company started moving west toward Highway 7, an Iraqi Fedayeen militiaman hiding in the village opened up with an AK-47, firing at Third Platoon only 50 meters away. A Marine returned fire, killing the Iraqi with 2 rounds. Then a number of Fedayeen opened up from the village and a line of trees and houses that ran north. Golf was quickly engaged in what Ross would later term "a classic spoiling attack by the Iraqis." Everyone hit the ground and moved 180 degrees around to face into the direction of fire. Hundreds of machine gun rounds with intermittent green tracers now whipped past them. "For the first few minutes, we didn't get a shot off," David said. "We were moving to get into positions."

Gunny Sweeney reacted quickly. "Nobody panic!" he yelled, then ran west away from Second Platoon. "We yelled over the fire, 'Where's he going?'" David recalled. Sweeney then jumped into a Humvee equipped with an MK-19 grenade launcher, rotated the weapon toward the village and began firing downrange. David could hear the *thump, thump, thump* sound as Sweeney fired the grenades off, which then started exploding in the tree line and buildings where the Fedayeen were situated. Sweeney's exploit fired up the men of Golf. "We started shouting," David said.

Ross then quickly barked orders to set his men up to attack the enemy positions. Campbell's First Squad-Second Platoon was ordered to cross an open field to the north to set up flanking fire from a tree line there. The rest of Second Platoon along with First and Third platoons formed a line near a solitary farmhouse, parallel to the Fedayeen positions. The CAAT sections moved in toward the infantry platoons and Weapons Platoon sighted in their mortars, AT4 rockets and machine guns. Nobody from Golf had been hit, despite being under enemy fire for about seven minutes.

Campbell's squad spread out and coordinated rushing lanes for their sprint across the open field. David was first up, and sprinted full speed across the exposed 200 meters toward the northern tree line as the rest of the squad laid down covering fire. "I never ran so fast in my life. I had an adrenaline sprint," David said later. "I could hear the bullets whipping by me, and see tracer fire, but I just kept running as fast as I could."

Reaching the tree line, David opened up with his machine gun to provide cover for the rest of the squad. "It was important to get a good base of fire going with my SAW," he said. While he provided fire, the eight other men of the squad—Campbell, Wilkens, Torres, Manin, Bicca, Flaminia, Perez, and Hone—all made it to the tree line, running with their full combat packs of almost 80 pounds, without one man being hit. "Guys told me after the battle they saw tracer bullets curve over and around my head, missing me," David said. "It was miraculous. Running in the open, not getting hit—the Lord really protected us."

When the squad reached cover in the tree line, they quickly set their weapons and opened up on the Fedayeen. The Iraqis kept firing back at Campbell's squad for some time, as they were probably beginning to realize that Golf Company had started to hem them in and attain superior firing positions. A tree not more than a foot away from David was hit with several enemy machine gun rounds, but not a single bullet or even a wood splinter hit him or any others in the squad. David fired bursts where he saw enemy muzzle flashes. By now all of Golf had opened up on the Fedayeen. Mortar rounds, rockets, grenades, machine guns, and M-16 rifle bullets brought a tremendous amount of fire on the enemy positions. Trees fell over from the explosions. So much dust, smoke, and debris came off the buildings and houses it was hard for the Marines on the ground to see targets clearly. The attached sniper teams had climbed onto the roof of the solitary farmhouse and were picking off Fedayeen.

After about a half hour of fire from Golf, the smoke started to clear, and David began firing at silhouettes he could see in the buildings. Sometime later, after Fedayeen fire had diminished, it wasn't clear to Ross whether the surviving Fedayeen were retreating or relocating their positions, a favorite tactic. The Fedayeen liked to preposition weapons over several locations, then begin firing, drop their weapons when empty and run to the next position, typically in an adjacent building, start firing again from the new position, and so on.

Ross wanted to finish the battle. He ordered Campbell's squad to sweep south, behind the CAAT sections and platoon positions, and swing east and then north to come up behind the Fedayeen positions and begin clearing house to house. As First Squad-Second Platoon moved south they ran into a muddy stream. Not wanting to waste time finding a shallow stream depth, David picked a spot and began to cross. The squad ended up having to carry their weapons above their heads as the water level reached chest high.

As they moved into the village and started to clear buildings, it became obvious that Golf had already decimated the Fedayeen. Not one Iraqi fighter was found alive. It was a grisly scene. David estimated he saw more than twenty dead, with body parts strewn all over. There were signs of several wounded having been dragged out, and judging from the size of the bloody trails many of those probably died as well. It was a big victory for Golf Company. Miraculously not one Marine from Golf had been wounded, not even a scratch. And there was quite possibly a measure of reckoning involved. Because Golf's position was close to where 507th Company had been ambushed the day before, it is very likely that some of the Iraqis involved in this firefight had been participants in the fight with the 507th.

After the fight was over for Golf, 1st Lt. Carl Havens, the company's weapons platoon commander, said to Ross, "You know, sir, I don't think your wife would appreciate it if she knew you were in the open so much during the fight!" Throughout the action, Ross was so intent on positioning his Marines and commanding his company that he had ignored the bullets and RPG rounds flying around him. He wasn't intentionally tempting fate; he was focused on making the right decisions to ensure his Marines would obtain every advantage possible. God had honored his courage and concern for his men by covering him with an undeniable shield of protection.

It is difficult for most of us who will never experience combat to even imagine what effect viewing such carnage could have upon the spirit, heart, and soul. And yet these young warriors must learn quickly to deal with such scenes that are often daily occurrences. Some harden their hearts; others internalize and bury feelings, seeking to put it out of their thoughts; a few draw back and have immediate difficulty dealing with the experience. None of us can truly predict how any given person seeing combat for the first time will respond. But God does know the effects on an individual basis and deeply cares for those involved.

During both the preparation for Operation Iraqi Freedom and the war itself, God's Holy Spirit moved on many believers in the United States to pray specifically for the hearts and minds of the men and women in combat. Among the family members of 2/8 troops, many believers were moved to call upon the Lord to guard and protect the inner man of these Marines. John Cain's parents, John and Ruth; his sisters Jennifer Peterson and Rebecca Redman; a friend from my work, Sean Biggs; our family friend Erin Hawkins and her mother, Connie; and our family all prayed often for God to protect hearts and minds. Without question hundreds of other believers were praying the same for 2/8. Physical protection is important, but even more important is the inner man. Wives and families also provided spiritual support for their Marines beyond prayer. First Lt. Chad Ragan, the assistant S3 operations officer for 2/8, was a perfect example of this. His wife, Becky, regularly sent Scripture quotes on three-by-five cards in her letters, which Chad found very helpful. With the help of God, the vast majority of 2/8 Marines, especially believers, handled the combat well and fully adjusted to normal life upon their return from Iraq later in 2003.

The attack on 2/8 that afternoon turned out to be much larger than just Golf Company's firefight. Within seconds after the start of Golf's firefight, the other 2/8 Rifle Companies—Echo and Fox—made contact with the enemy. The Iraqis had started what would prove to be their only coordinated large scale simultaneous attack on 2/8 and RCT-2 during the war. Echo Company was in contact with direct enemy fire from the west and from north of the Euphrates River, and would remain engaged for the rest of the afternoon. Fox Company started receiving direct fire from the north side of the Euphrates River and from within the hospital to the east, as well as indirect mortar and artillery fire. The Iraqis had managed to sneak a machine gun into some weeds on the north side of the Euphrates River directly across from Fox's positions, and they were sweeping the air above Fox's positions with bullets. The machine gun and indirect fire onto Fox's positions quickly became very heavy, causing every Marine, including the observing senior officers, at the Euphrates Bridge to head for cover.

Given that all three Rifle Companies were engaged in combat, with their radiomen and whip-antenna backpacks moving around, Fulford at TAC CP was not able to maintain continuous communications with the companies. But good fortune prevailed. Mortenson's command Humvee carried a high-power radio, and because his location at the Euphrates bridge was close to all three Rifle Companies, he was able to speak continuously with all three and with Fulford in TAC. Working in tag-team fashion for the two-hour duration of the fight, Mortenson relayed requests for fire support from Yeo, Dremann, and Ross to TAC and was then able to discuss details, clear requests with Fulford, and transmit messages back to the rifle company commanders. The seemingly innocuous visit to Fox Company to meet up with his rifle company commanders and superior officers had turned into an incredibly providential event. Mortenson was able to effectively command his battalion from his Humvee at the bridge.

Within Fox Company, 1st Sgt. Gatewood would later recall, "It felt like all hell broke loose. We were receiving incoming fire from three directions." As the enemy fire quickly escalated, Gatewood remembers having two distinct thoughts: *The Iraqis are trying to hem 2/8 in and surround us*, and, *We're not all going to make it out of here.* The intensity of the incoming fire was so severe that even a seasoned combat veteran like Gatewood thought 2/8 Marines would die that afternoon.

Early during the fight, 2/8 and Fox received their first casualty of the war when Lcpl. Josh Menard of Houston, Texas, received a shrapnel wound in the palm of his left hand. Menard was positioned on the Euphrates bridge, and an incoming AK-47 round hit his SAW weapon, creating a chunk of shrapnel that hit his hand. Hearing of his casualty over the radio, Mortenson began calling to get Menard out. The fighting was so involved, the response back was, "Sir, we can't get him out. We can't disengage." Mortenson then began personally to set an evacuation action in motion. He called for an LAV vehicle to come forward onto the bridge to remove Menard, and then jumped in his Humvee and drove onto the bridge in the midst of incoming fire. Arriving before the LAV, Mortenson placed his Humvee between the incoming fire and Menard to create a shield. When the LAV arrived, Mortenson helped load Menard into the vehicle, and the LAV and Mortenson moved south back to the base of the bridge.

Mortenson had also called for the forward battalion aid station (BAS) to move up to the bridge, and he and the corpsmen set up triage and treated Menard right there at the bridge. Mortenson's coolness under fire and demonstrated concern for his Marines above his own personal safety brought a huge measure of encouragement to his men. Menard would later tell his family that the positive effect on Fox Company morale from Mortenson's actions was incredible.

Soon after the fight started for Fox Company, acts of miraculous protection and individual heroism began to take place. Minutes into the fight, First Platoon Staff Sgt. St. John and the platoon radio operator, Lcpl. Clay, were standing next to a stone alcove near a farmhouse when a mortar round hit. Both men were blown several feet into the air but somehow landed on their feet and started running. Just seconds later, a second mortar round exploded, catapulting both men thirty feet through the air and dropping them flat on the ground. Watching the whole event, Gatewood thought for sure Clay and St. John had been killed. *They're gone*, he thought. Miraculously, not only were both men alive, but both stood to their feet. St. John hadn't been injured at all, and Clay had suffered a concussion and a shrapnel wound to his leg and would later be diagnosed with a C-spine injury.

Disoriented by the concussion Clay began wandering aimlessly into an open field, directly into the area where enemy machine-gun fire, mortars, and artillery rounds were landing. Seeing all this, his fellow Marines reacted heroically. Situated to the east of Clay by about 150 meters, Cpl. John Friend, squad leader of Second Squad-Third Platoon, happened to be repositioning with his platoon toward a tree line standing between them and Clay. Friend witnessed both mortar explosions, and seeing Clay beginning to wander, he took off and ran toward Clay and St. John, braving the machine-gun and indirect fire. Lcpl. Lugo from Friend's squad also saw Clay in danger and he too left his position and sprinted the 150 meters to Clay.

By the time Friend and Lugo arrived, Clay had fallen down and St. John was kneeling over him. S. Sgt. Russell of Third Platoon arrived soon after Friend and Lugo and started checking on St. John while Lugo placed Clay's radio on his back and Friend picked up Clay and laid him on his back. Russell, St. John and Friend, with Clay on his back, then began to run toward the company casualty collection point, about 100 meters away. Lugo peeled off toward First Platoon's position to bring Clay's radio to 2nd Lt. Wong, the First Platoon CO. While in transit, Cpl. Armeged of Weapons Platoon ran over and joined Friend to assist in carrying Clay to the casualty collection point.

At the collection point, it was clear that St. John was perfectly fine and required no medical aid, so he left to get right back into the fight. Throughout the rescue of Lcpl. Clay, Iraqi machine-gun, mortar, and artillery rounds continually landed within Fox Company's positions. "Things were still going on pretty heavy the whole time," Friend would later recall. For his bravery and heroic actions under fire, Friend was awarded the Bronze Star.

Mortenson had the forward BAS set up at the base of the bridge, which was not more than 20 feet from Fox Company's 60 mm mortar pit. Mortenson and Fox Marines then repositioned the company's seven-ton trucks between the incoming enemy fire and the casualty collection point, to shield the wounded. As Menard was attended to, Clay was brought in and placed on a stretcher. In between radio contacts, Mortenson was able to walk over and talk to his wounded Marines. Seeing his battalion commander standing over him, Clay entreated him to send him back to his squad. Although moved by Clay's show of determination and esprit de corps, Mortenson knew Clay needed to be evacuated. Mortenson later said, "Clay kept saying, 'Sir, send me back, send me back!'" Seeking to put Clay at ease, he began to joke with him. Mortenson said: "Look, Clay, you're bleeding all over my [expletive] stretcher. You're going to go back—we'll plug up all your holes and bring you right back." Clay laughed at that.

About five minutes after St. John's and Clay's miraculous encounter, another miracle took place. An incoming Iraqi mortar round was heading straight for Fox's 60 mm mortar pit, where the casualty collection point with Mortenson and crew were just feet away. The incoming round hit an overhead power line and exploded above the pit. The explosion broke the high-voltage line, which swung clear of the pit and the collection point and landed about 10 feet away from their positions. According to 1st Sergeant Gatewood, who later recalled the event, had the mortar round missed the power line, it would have landed in the pit and wiped out the four Marines there—the three-man mortar crew and S. Sgt. Charles Allen.

Certainly the Marines teach their officers and company sergeants how to cleverly set up large placements like mortar pits so that they will be protected as much as possible against incoming rounds, but no amount of calculation and savvy on the part of Dremann and Gatewood would have convinced them to count on an overhead power line as protection. God had provided another miracle. He not only made sure the Iraqi round hit the power line, but He also made sure the broken power line landed clear of the Fox Marines.

Despite the heavy incoming fire, the Marines began hitting back with vigor. Responding to a Fox Company call for air support to knock out the menacing Iraqi machine gun in the weeds north of the river, a Marine Huey helicopter gunship destroyed the gun position about twenty to thirty minutes into the fight. Firing two SMAW rockets and using fire from SAW machine guns and M-16s, the First Squad from Wong's First Platoon destroyed a boathouse across the river that was being used as a base of fire by the Iraqis.

Fox's 60 mm mortars were landing on the eastern hospital, firing back at the Iraqis who were using the hospital for cover. Mortenson had moved several Light Armored Vehicles (LAVs) with their deadly 25 mm guns up onto the high point of the

Euphrates bridge. The LAVs were pounding Iraqi positions on the north side of the river in front of both Fox's and Echo's positions. Counter-battery radar from Starnes' 1/10 began identifying sources of incoming Iraqi fire to the east, north, and west of 2/8, and his big 155 mm guns began taking their toll.

During the fight, quick action on the part of Fulford in TAC prevented a friendly fire incident from occurring. The call came in over the RCT-2 network for "red rain," the call sign for a counter-battery fire mission within the 2/8 sector. All fire missions in a given battalion's area of responsibility need to be cleared and approved by the TAC CP. Fulford checked the coordinates and realized the intended fire would land right on Fox Company's 60 mm mortars. The 1/10 counter-battery radar was picking up Dremann's mortars firing at the eastern hospital, and his incoming mortars were thought to be Iraqi. Fulford caught the targeting error and cancelled the red rain.

Had even one 155 mm round landed anywhere near Fox's mortar pit, it would have wiped out the pit, Mortenson, Dupree, and the Marines in the BAS and the casualty collection point. Mortenson later explained, "This was very early in the fight. We were not as good at this moment as we were going to be 24 hours from then. Combat is a huge learning curve."

While the fight raged, three more Fox Marines experienced miraculous protection. Cpl. Diazmartinez, Lcpl. Murphy and Pfc. Pienta were also thrown through the air from the explosions of Iraqi rounds. Like S. Sgt. St. John, they all landed without a scratch, with no wounds from shrapnel and no shell shock. Throughout the course of the battle, just two more casualties would occur within Fox Company's position. Lcpl. Santa Maria and a Navy corpsman received shrapnel wounds from Iraqi mortars. In a fierce fight that lasted two hours, a total of three Marines and one Navy corpsman had been injured. No Americans died and none were missing in action.

The firefight ended in the late afternoon just before sundown. During the evening, 2/8 Marines were able to reflect on what they had just been through. Lt. Wong wryly remarked to S. Sgt. St. John, "Interesting day. I'd like to see us top this." Clearly Fox Company had experienced miraculous protection from the Lord. Capt. Dremann would later state, "We had a bunch of Marines that should have died that day but didn't. At one point we had over 10 rounds of heavy Iraqi artillery rounds land in rapid succession right on top of our position, but nobody died."

Chaplain Rogers had come up to Fox and prayed over the four wounded Marines. He was amazed. "I never had to use oil to anoint them," he recalled. Fulford would later call these miraculous events just one set of many over the first five days in An-Nasiriyah that could be explained only by the protection of God. And 1st Sgt. Gatewood was still amazed months after the battle. "I know for a fact there was divine intervention here, no doubt," Gatewood said, and to emphasize his point, added, "I'm still baffled by how those guys survived!" With characteristic intensity, he was still incredulous about the Iraqis' sneaking a machine gun across the river from Fox's position. "I still don't know how those Iraqis got that machine gun in those weeds without us seeing them!" he exclaimed.

Although the Iraqis were successful at executing off this one well-coordinated attack, using mortar and artillery rounds, it would be their last major attack upon Fox. Throughout the late afternoon on the 24th, Starnes' counter-battery fire destroyed the Iraqi guns. For the next few days the Iraqis would manage to fire only an occasional mortar or artillery round. After March 27, Iraqi artillery and mortars had been effectively wiped out.

In spite of the intense two-hour fight, Mortenson and Fulford had not forgotten the eastern hospital. During the battle, they had been re-planning their attack on the facility. It had become evident that it was a stronghold of the enemy. "The largest volume of fire against the battalion was emanating from the hospital, on both Fox and Golf," Mortenson said later. He had begun executing mortar barrages in support of the anticipated attack by Fox and Golf Companies. Initially firing Fox's 60 mm mortars, he then upped the intensity by adding Weapons Company's 81 mm mortars into the fire missions. When twenty-five to thirty rounds of 81s had been fired into the hospital, Iraqi soldiers began running out of the building. Many were gunned down by Marines from both Fox and 2nd Lt. Bouza's First Platoon of Golf Company. Several were captured.

In the late afternoon, Mortenson coordinated with Starnes and 1/10 to add an artillery barrage of the hospital. Just minutes before 1/10 was to commence their attack, Task Force Tarawa G3, Col. Johnson, who was still at the bridge, informed Mortenson to stop his attack on the hospital. Johnson told him that Task Force Tarawa intelligence had concluded American POWs might still be in the hospital and that U.S. Special Forces might be getting involved.

By the time the sun set on March 24, the Iraqi attacks on 2/8 had been thoroughly crushed. Golf Company moved back into its original defensive perimeter of the previous evening. Around dusk, an Iraqi tank had engaged MacCutcheon's CAAT Platoon south of Golf's position and was destroyed. Marine artillery from 1/10 also destroyed some Iraqi supporting elements in the vicinity of the tank. Fox and Golf both fired upon some minor Iraqi elements that evening, but neither was engaged in major fighting.

Evidently the late afternoon mortar attacks from 2/8 did more that just destroy enemy targets in and around the hospital and flush out Iraqi soldiers. They had also convinced most of the remaining Iraqi soldiers that their chances of survival were slim if they remained there. In the early evening, around twilight, a convoy of three vehicles attempted to leave the hospital grounds. They were intercepted and stopped by squads from Fox and Golf. Dupree and his team initially focused on what looked like two physicians—men wearing white lab coats—and began interrogating them.

At first, the so-called doctors claimed they were non-military physicians and that they were evacuating wounded civilians. Searches of the vehicles turned up some AK-47s. More important, the vehicles also contained about twenty Iraqi men, almost all military-aged, some wearing uniforms under lab coats. Many of them were wounded, a few severely. The two "doctors" turned out to be a military physician and an Iraqi general. The wounded Iraqi men obviously were soldiers who had been injured fighting 2/8. Dupree sent the severely wounded soldiers to the BAS, but he kept interrogating the doctor and general for another two hours.

The doctor spoke English well, and he claimed to have attended to Jessica Lynch. Apparently she was suffering from concussion and broken bones after an RPG round hit her vehicle during the ambush on the 23rd. Dupree then set up a database to record Lynch's injuries based on the doctor's testimony. The information would help later, if Lynch was rescued, to determine if she had additional wounds and, thus, had been mistreated by the Iraqis. The doctor told interrogators that Lynch and other American POWs had been moved to the Saddam Hospital on the western side of An-Nasiriyah.

Dupree then asked him two last questions. "Any civilians or wounded left?" The doctor answered, "No. We're abandoning the hospital." "Are there any soldiers left?" Dupree asked. "No soldiers left," the doctor responded. Some sniping could be heard coming from the upper floors of the hospital. "So who's shooting at us?" Dupree countered. "No one is shooting at you," the doctor replied. Clearly, not only was the doctor lying, but the remaining Iraqis in the hospital would need to be dealt with.

Throughout the day of the 24th, Kerry Sanders and his NBC-TV crew were also braving the incoming fire and managed to send off live reports of 2/8's firefights back to the United States. Around 6 p.m. Iraqi time, or 10 a.m. Eastern Time, Sanders was giving a live report for NBC's *Today* show when Fox Company's wounded were carried right behind him on stretchers. Just minutes later Sanders managed to videotape an interview with Lcpl. Josh Menard—and then Sanders thoughtfully let the young Marine call home using Sanders' satellite phone, not realizing his cameraman was still videotaping.

Menard called his mother, Elizabeth, a nurse, at about 9:15 a.m. in Houston. Normally, Elizabeth would have left for work by that time, but she had been up much of the night watching the news for more information about casualties from 1/2 and Task Force Tarawa. What started as a humanitarian gesture on Sanders' part turned into one of the great images and news stories of the war. America watched and listened as Josh sat on his stretcher talking to and reassuring his mother, who added her good prognosis to their conversation.

The dramatic story set off a huge response within Elizabeth's
d Joshua's circle of friends and families. Since before the war,
ɔsh's picture had been posted on prayer boards in numerous
ɪurches. Dozens of friends, family members, and acquaintances
who had been lifting up Josh and 2/8 in prayer began calling
Elizabeth. About an hour after her talk with Josh, Mortenson's
wife, Leeann, called to offer her support. A little while later, Dremann's wife, Catherine, called Elizabeth to comfort her and then
Judy Johnson, the mother of Lcpl. David Johnson called and told
her about the prayer groups involving the wives and families of
2/8 Marines. Elizabeth was eager to get involved with the prayer
groups and subsequently did so. Catherine Dremann also began
calling daily to check in with her and also direct her through
appropriate channels to secure updated information concerning
Josh. The immensity of the heartfelt support and the knowledge
that so many people were praying for her and her son were almost
overwhelming for Elizabeth. Reflecting on the events later, she
stated, "I witnessed firsthand how much these Marines care for
each other."

One moving story of a believer strongly led by the Holy Spirit
to pray for Joshua Menard involved a friend named Ben Shook.
Ben grew up with Josh in Houston, Texas, and was involved in a
missions trip to Mexico in March when the war broke out. Over
the night of March 23 while in Tlaxiaco, Mexico, around 2 a.m.
local time, which was 11 a.m. in Iraq on the 24th, Ben was awakened with an overwhelming burden to pray for his friend Josh.
"The Holy Spirit kept repeating to me, 'You need to pray for Josh,'"
Ben recalled. "The Holy Spirit was saying, 'You need to keep praying for him—now—seriously!' It was unlike any other prayer I've
ever had. It was so intense, it became emotional. This continued
for over 45 minutes." True to the words spoken in churches before
the start of the war, God had awakened this young man to pray a
protective prayer. Unknown to Ben, just a few hours later Josh was
wounded, but frankly, just as easily, Josh could have been killed.
Certainly the Iraqi soldier shooting at Josh was not aiming for his
rifle, but that's where the bullet landed. Three days later, on March
27, Ben was informed by fellow missionaries who had received

an e-mail from Ben's mother that a friend of his had been shot, and that the friend was not killed, just wounded. Immediately Ben stated, "It was Josh Menard; I know it was Josh." Later that day Ben was able to confirm in another e-mail from his mother that indeed Josh had been wounded in the hand, to the amazement of his fellow missionaries. Only when Ben arrived back in Houston on March 30, however, did he learn how big a deal Josh Menard's story had become.

The first news of casualties always has a chilling effect on families and friends back home, and it must be especially tough on the wives of commanding officers. Without doubt these wives gain a personal interest in the Marines under the command of their husbands, and even if their husbands are unharmed the news of casualties hits home like family. When the reports of Fox Company wounded first came in, Catherine Dremann initially in her words "felt frozen," in part because she wasn't sure just who and how many had become casualties. Knowing her husband's company was in heavy fighting, she paced up and down in their home on base at Camp Lejeune for a time, then found her rosary and went to her knees in prayer. "The rote prayers were the only thing I could remember to pray, the only thing that could slow my heart and mind down and bring peace," she recalled later. Soon, dozens of friends and family members began calling. "The phone never quit ringing, with some calls from people I'd never expected would call," Catherine recalled. She received a phone call from the mother of a childhood friend, who told Catherine she was praying for her. One of Capt. Dremann's former company commanders, now out of the Corps, Brian Jimenez, called specifically to comfort and to pray with Catherine over the phone. Jimenez subsequently called to pray with Catherine once a week until the end of the war.

If Catherine Dremann was in need of relief from the tension of the day, almost as if right on cue her older son provided it. Later in the evening of the 24th, Catherine was getting ready to pray as she did every night with her two children before putting them to bed. Her five-year-old son, Jackson, was noticeably uneasy, which was a bit unusual for him. He asked his mother if he could hold a picture of his daddy before they prayed, and Catherine obliged her thoughtful son. People had been telling Jackson all his young life that he looked just like his father, and he asked his mother whether Jesus was still watching over Daddy. Catherine reassured him that Jesus was, because Daddy was doing an important thing in fighting the bad guys. After a thoughtful pause, Jackson spoke his concern. "Yes, but Mom, I'm worried. We look so much alike, Jesus might get us confused!" Restraining herself from laughing over her son's ingenuous concern, Catherine lovingly told him that Jesus doesn't get mixed up and that He is going to be able to tell the difference. Jackson went to bed satisfied.

Back in An-Nasiriyah, as the eventful second day had come to an end, the course of the battle for the city had already taken a sharp turn. Task Force Tarawa and 2/8 had repulsed and destroyed everything that had been thrown at them. The Third U.S. Army, the unit within U.S. Central Command in charge of all ground forces for Operation Iraqi Freedom, later reported that the Iraqi counter-attacks against RCT-2 on March 24 included a brigade-sized force—meaning 4,000 or more enemy soldiers were involved. With what can be described only as miraculous intervention from God, 2/8 had sustained a total of just four wounded, whereas Iraqi losses had been very high. In two days of fighting for An-Nasiriyah, the tally was now mounting fast in favor of Task Force Tarawa and 2/8.

Official USMC portrait of Lt. Col. Royal Mortenson, 2/8 Commanding Officer taken about one year before the start of Operation Iraqi Freedom.

Photo Credit: USMC

Photo Credit: Lt. Col. R. Mortenson

USS *Saipan* at dockside, Norfolk, Virginia, January 2003, awaiting Marines from 2/8 and Marine Air Group 29.

Photo Credit: Cpl. J. Cain

The calm before the storm. Two Marines silhouetted against an ocean sunset aboard the USS *Saipan*, en route to Kuwait.

Photo Credit: Lcpl. J. Randolfi

U.S. Navy task force carrying 2nd Marine Expeditionary Brigade, sailing to Kuwait, January 2003.

Photo Credit: Cpl. D. Rodriguez

USS *Saipan* passing through the Suez Canal on route to Kuwait. Notice the machine gunner on duty.

Photo Credit: Cpl. D. Rodriguez

2/8 Marines (left to right) Lcpl. Ross, Lcpl. Rodriguez, Cpl. Garcia of Golf Company 2nd Platoon riding in a helicopter from the *Saipan* towards Kuwait, February 16, 2003.

Lcpl. Thomas and Lcpl. Rodriguez in "tent city," Camp Shoop, Kuwait, February 2003.

Photo Credit:
Cpl. D. Rodriguez

Photo Credit: Lt. Col. R. Mortenson

2/8 Marines relaxing at Camp Shoop, Kuwait, with a pickup baseball game, February, 2003.

Photo Credit: Lt. Col. R. Mortenson

Lt. Col. Mortenson with 2/8 Sergeant Major and Company Commanders: left to right: Capt. Yeo, Capt. Luciano, Mortenson, 1st Sgt. Thorne, Capt. Dremann, Capt. Ross, Capt. Ryans, Kuwait, February 2003

Photo Credit: Lt. Col. R. Mortenson

S3 Operations Officer Major Fulford in a light moment with Rifle Company Commanders: left to right: Capt. Yeo, Capt. Ross, Fulford, Capt. Dremann, Kuwait, March 2003.

Photo Credit: Lt. Col. R. Mortenson

Left to right: Capt. Dremann, Capt. Ross and Capt. Dupree, shortly before the start of Operation Iraqi Freedom, March 20th, 2003.

Photo Credit: Eric Feferberg/AFP/Getty Images

Battalion Commander Lt. Col. Royal Mortenson addresses 2/8 Marines the morning of their attack into Iraq, March 20ᵗʰ, 2003.

COMBAT

Photo Credit: Cpl. J. Cain

CAAT Platoon encounters burning oil wells, set ablaze by retreating Iraqi forces, dusk, March 20th or 21st, 2003.

Photo Credit: Cpl. D. Rodriguez

First day of combat in An-Nasiriyah, March 23rd, 2003. An Iraqi tank burns in the middle of the image. The view is from a Golf Company, 2nd Platoon 7-ton truck.

Photo Credit: Cpl. D. Rodriguez

An-Nasiriyah, March 23rd, 2003. An Iraqi Army vehicle burns in the distance. The view is from a Golf Company 2nd Platoon truck looking out past a machine gun.

Photo Credit: Lcpl. J. Randolfi

Pfc. Randolfi and Cpl. Blackman from Weapons Platoon, Golf Company ride into An-Nasiriyah locked, loaded, and ready, March 23rd, 2003.

Photo Credit: Eric Feferberg/AFP/Getty Images

2/8 Marines advance under fire, An-Nasiriyah, sometime between March 23rd and March 31st, 2003.

Photo Credit: Eric Feferberg/AFP/Getty Images

2/8 Marines firing upon Iraqi positions, An-Nasiriyah, sometime between March 23rd and March 31st, 2003.

Photo Credit: Eric Feferberg/AFP/Getty Images

2/8 Marines engaged in urban warfare, An-Nasiriyah, late March 2003.

Photo Credit: Eric Feferberg/AFP/Getty Images

A Weapons Company mortar team from 2/8 fires upon Iraqi positions, sometime around March 26th, 2003.

Photo Credit: Cpl. D. Rodriguez

March 26th, 2003 in An-Nasiriyah, the day after torrential rains the night of the 25th. Lcpl. Aleman from Golf Company 2nd Platoon, not looking too cheerful.

Photo Credit: Eric Feferberg/AFP/Getty Images

2/8 Marines in a muddy fighting hole, March 26th, 2003. The rain-softened ground would providentially prove life-saving later that night.

Photo Credit: Eric Feferberg/AFP/Getty Images

A view of 2/8's Main CP the morning of March 27th, 2003 after the evening firefight of the 26th in An-Nasiriyah. Despite the carnage, miraculously no 2/8 Marines or attached Navy personnel were killed.

Photo Credit: Lcpl. J. Randolfi

A Marine from Weapons Platoon, Golf Company catches some daytime sleep while still in his chemical warfare protective suit. March 2003, An-Nasiriyah.

Photo Credit: Lt. Col. R. Mortenson

Lt. Col. Mortenson in his TAC CP, an abandoned building, in An-Nasiriyah, March 2003.

Photo Credit: Lt. Col. R. Mortenson

A Scout-Sniper team from 2/8 about to leave on a patrol, An-Nasiriyah, sometime between March 24th and 31st, 2003.

Photo Credit: Cpl. J. Cain

2/8 Marines from CAAT section Gold, March 2003, somewhere in and around An-Nasiriyah. Despite frequent engagements with enemy forces, incredibly no CAAT Platoon vehicles were disabled and no casualties were taken from enemy fire during Operation Iraqi Freedom

Photo Credit: Cpl. J. Cain

Lcpl. Cain from CAAT section Gold at the wheel of a HMMWV, or "Humvee," Iraq, March 2003.

Photo Credit: Eric Feferberg/AFP/Getty Images

The unfortunate victims of war: an Iraqi woman pleads for help for her wounded husband. "Docs" from 2/8—Navy Corpmen—treated his wounds.

Photo Credit: Eric Feferberg/AFP/Getty Images

A battery of 155 millimeter artillery from 1st Battalion, 10th Marines, Task Force Tarawa, near An-Nasiriyah, March 2003. 1/10 artillery was devastatingly effective against Iraqi forces throughout Operation Iraqi Freedom.

Photo Credit: Lcpl. J. Randolfi

Winning hearts and minds. A Golf Company patrol befriended this Iraqi family. April 2003. Lcpl. Rodriguez on far right.

Photo Credit: Cpl. J. Cain

Not an uncommon scene. Camels roam the land, southern Iraq, April 2003.

Photo Credit: Cpl. J. Cain

A common scene. An Iraqi bunker, with unused ordnance strewn all over. View looking through the front window of a 2/8 CAAT team Humvee.

Evidence of Saddam Hussein's organized malice toward Jews. This pistol range target was found by 2/8 Marines in an Iraq Army/terrorist training camp overrun by the battalion. The Arabic inscription reads, "This is a Jew."

Photo Credit:
Major R. Fulford

Photo Credit: Eric Feferberg/AFP/Getty Images

2/8 Marines inventory a small part of the huge Iraqi weapons and ammunition depot found at Ad-Diwaneyah, early April, 2003.

Photo Credit: Lcpl. J. Randolfi

A group photo of part of the Task Force "Rebel," the rapid reaction mobile reserve commanded by Major Alford in Al-Kut, used to help restore order and civil function to the city. April–May 2003.

Photo Credit: Cpl. D. Rodriguez

Their combat over, Brig. Gen. R. Natonski, CO of Task Force Tarawa, left, with Lcpl. Rodriguez back in Kuwait, mid-May, 2003. On the right are Cpls. "Ski" and Zenk of 1st Platoon, Golf Company.

Photo Credit: Cpl. D. Rodriguez

One happy day, May 12th, 2003. 2/8 Marines from Golf Company about to ride into the well deck of the USS *Saipan* and embark for the trip home.

Photo Credit: Lt. Col. R. Mortenson

The look of thankfulness and a job well done. Capt. Ross and 1st Sgt. Beith of Golf Company, back aboard the USS *Saipan*, May 2003.

Photo Credit: Cpl. J. Cain

U.S. Navy ships carrying 2/8 and Task Force Tarawa Marines heading for home. May 2003.

Photo Credit: G. Thomas

Family and friends at Camp Lejeune mob the busses carrying their 2/8 Marines, June 22nd, 2003.

Photo Credit: J. Alford

Fox Company CO Capt. Rich Dremann and wife Catherine re-unite at homecoming, Camp Lejeune, June 22, 2003.

Photo Credit: G. Thomas

Golf Company Marines Cpl. Perez (left) and Lcpl. David Thomas (right) of 1st Squad, 2nd Platoon pose weapons and all at their homecoming.

Photo Credit: G. Thomas

Lcpl. Erik Ross of Golf Company, happy to be home, Camp Lejeune, June 22, 2003.

Photo Credit: G. Thomas

Lcpl. Brad Ruetschi at the 2/8 homecoming. No mistaking his smile.

Photo Credit: J. Alford

Kerry Sanders of NBC News (right) interviews Major Alford, 2/8 homecoming at Camp Lejeune, June 22, 2003. NBC cameraman Sebastian
Rich is on the left.

6

AN-NASIRIYAH:
MARCH 25 TO MARCH 26

Let them be confounded and dismayed forever; yes, let them be put to shame and perish, that they may know that You, whose name alone is the LORD, are the Most High over all the earth.
—PSALM 83:17-18

Audacity, and not caution, must be our watchword.
—J.F.C. FULLER, FROM *LEADING MARINES*

EARLY IN THE MORNING OF Tuesday, March 25, in Iraq, starting around 2 a.m., a major sandstorm began to make its way into An-Nasiriyah. Sandstorms had been building up north and east of the city for the past day or so, causing some delay in the advance of the I MEF and Third ID. During the early evening of March 24 in the eastern United States, right about the time the sandstorm started entering An-Nasiriyah, the American TV news networks were reporting excerpts about the storms from Al-Jezeerah and other Arab news organizations. The Arab networks were broadcasting Iraqi citizens in Baghdad who were claiming that Allah was fighting for them by sending the sandstorms. The Holy Spirit within each of us watching started to rise up. Pam and I started praying, "Lord, use these sandstorms for Your glory, then cause them to dry up at their source!" Our family friend Erin was praying exactly the same prayer at her home at approximately the same time, as likely were thousands of other Christians across America. The answer to these prayers would come quickly.

Back in An-Nasiriyah, the morning saw the First Marine Regiment transiting through the city along Highway 7, to head north and help spearhead the I MEF attack through the heart of Iraq and eventually into Baghdad. Early in the morning, Mortenson had received clearance from Task Force Tarawa headquarters to take the hospital. Intelligence had concluded that Americans were no longer being held there. Fox Company was assigned as the lead unit in the attack with Golf Company in support. However, Mortenson could not release Fox and Golf to commence with the attack until the passage of the First Marines was completed, which didn't occur until approximately 1 p.m. due to the large size of the regiment.

The Iraqis had turned the hospital into a military stronghold, thus making it a legitimate target. Iraqi soldiers had been constantly sniping and shooting at 2/8 from within the building. Sandbags and fortifications were spread around the hospital compound, and there had been a constant stream of Iraqi combat vehicles in and out. Early in the morning of the 25th an Iraqi heavy machine-gun vehicle had entered the hospital compound. An Iraqi tank also was there. To the Marines, this eastern hospital represented just one of many examples of despicable and immoral tactics the Iraqis used throughout the fighting.

With the attack from Fox Company pending, Mortenson initiated a barrage, with both 60 mm and 81 mm mortars firing into the hospital compound to soften the Iraqi defenses. As the 1st Marines passed through the bridge, Fulford and Dremann were coordinating the attack plan down in TAC when one of Dremann's Javelin gunners spotted the Iraqi tank in the rear of the hospital. Thermal imaging revealed the tank's engine was not "hot," a sign that the tank wasn't planning to move anywhere soon—but the tank's gun remained a major threat to Fox. Fulford then asked Dremann how soon before he could "step off" and initiate the attack. Dremann said thirty minutes and Fulford ordered the attack. The plan called for Fox Company to attack the hospital moving west to east, with Golf Company to block any attempted Iraqi escape to the south and eastern rear areas of the compound.

Dremann chose 2nd Lt. Jeff Wong's First Platoon as the main effort for the company attack. Wong's platoon of three rifle squads was reinforced for the assault with a full machine-gun squad led by Sgt. Voelkel, an assault squad led by Cpl. Zonneveld and Sgt. Horton, and a fourth rifle squad—the First Squad from Third Platoon—led by Sgt. Stewart. The assault squad would use C4 explosives to create a breach in the fence surrounding the hospital. This would allow the rifle and machine-gun squads to sweep through into the hospital compound. The Second and Third Squads from Third Platoon were set up initially as a base of fire, positioned toward the bridge, ready to provide covering fire during First Platoon's assault. Dremann kept his Second Platoon back at the bridge to act as the rear guard during the attack. Because of his combat-engineering experience, 1st Sgt. Gatewood would also be in the lead assisting the assault squad with their efforts.

For the next thirty minutes Fox Company scrambled to prepare for the attack. "Gunny Hall did three to four hours work in that thirty minutes," Dremann later explained. Hall pulled his Humvee to Wong's position, and the Marines loaded up on grenades, extra ammo, and explosives. Even with the well-conceived plan of Dremann, the attack loomed ominously. The terrain between Wong's position and the hospital was an open field of some 300 meters which provided no cover for the Marines. They would be open targets for the Iraqis in the hospital as they advanced their attack directly into the firing positions of the concealed enemy gunners.

But God provided a miracle of protection once again. As the attack commenced exactly thirty minutes after Fulford's order, the sandstorm hit in full force and covered Dremann's Marines. Dremann later stated, "At 30 minutes precisely we stepped off, and the sandstorm kicked up. The clear day turned hazy, and we couldn't see the 300 meters to the hospital." Gatewood later recalled with amazement, "The sandstorm helped cover the attack. We were west of the hospital, with nothing but open field leading up to the hospital. I don't know how we would have gotten over across that field if it wasn't for the sandstorm!"

Wong recalled, "Here's a little divine intervention—on our little jog toward the berm, a thick fog rolled into the area. It was the weirdest thing I've ever seen. It obscured us from the hospital, and presumably from the sights of the enemy. People talked about the fog of war constantly, but I never thought I'd actually see it in action." And Cpl. Friend recalled, "Once the sandstorm kicked up, we had to stop our supporting fire. We couldn't see our own guys."

Perhaps a lesson from this miracle is that the Lord knows best. One good blinding sandstorm from God is better cover than a company of some of the most elite infantrymen in the world loaded with the best weapons money can buy. All of Wong's Marines made it to the outer berm of the hospital compound without a single casualty. Clearly God was answering the prayers of His people.

The first breach attempt failed because not enough explosives were used. The second time, Zonneveld and Horton didn't take a chance—they used an entire stick of C4 on the fence. Wong later remarked, "When that thing went off, you could probably hear the boom back at Lejeune!" Wong's Marines swept into the compound without hesitation, with Voelkel's machine gun teams laying withering fire onto enemy positions as the rifle squads advanced. The Iraqis had built several outer buildings west and south of the main hospital building that needed to be cleared before the hospital itself could be taken. Gatewood later described this part of the attack. "There were several ante-buildings.... They were obviously built and positioned for defense of the hospital.... We found Iraqis in some of the buildings, mostly snipers, and killed most of them."

When their men got to the main three-story hospital building, Dremann and Gatewood coordinated simultaneous squad attacks on each level. Fox secured the hospital but still was receiving some incoming sniping. A few Iraqis had managed to avoid getting caught in the attack and had taken a position in a stucco building east of the hospital, still wanting to fight. Dremann came up with a bright idea to deal with them. He took every Fox Company Marine carrying the M203 grenade launcher—about thirty Marines—and had each of them fire four or five grenades into the stucco building. The structure was obliterated. The sniping was quickly silenced. A search of the building later revealed that no Iraqi soldier had survived the barrage.

The sacking of the hospital revealed a large cache of Iraqi arms. Gatewood recalled, "We were surprised at the amount of weapons found, preloaded and cleaned, ready to be fired. Plus, we found 3,000 chemical warfare suits." Fox also found hundreds of atropine sticks, used to prevent heart seizure when exposed to chemical nerve agents, and a large supply of ammunition. It was such a large amount that it took almost five hours to completely clear the hospital, and gather and destroy all the weapons. Combat engineers from the Second Engineering Battalion assigned to 2/8 destroyed the weapons and later blew up the tank east of the hospital. Dremann's men also found several torture chambers in the hospital that were equipped with bedsprings with car batteries attached. Gatewood was disgusted. "Only a warped, despotic regime would use hospitals as cover for military and torture operations," he later stated.

The attack was a major, hard-fought victory for 2/8 and Fox Company. Dremann would recall that "Fox Marines did some pretty brave and remarkable things" in this attack. Although it incurred no casualties in the advance across the field to the berm, Fox did receive a casualty when the second-to-last Marine through the breach, Cpl. Hammond, was shot in the calf. S. Sgt. St. John carried Hammond from the breach point to the company casualty collection point, some 50 meters away. Five other men received shrapnel wounds inside the main hospital building when a zealous Marine fired his M203 grenade launcher inside a corridor to try to blow open a locked gate. All things considered, Fox Company had incurred miraculously few casualties for such a difficult assault.

A thorough search of the hospital yielded more documents

and a major piece of intel: the discarded uniforms of Jessica Lynch and Lori Piestawa. Lynch's uniform had been surgically cut along the right leg, apparently to treat a leg wound, and there was a small amount of blood on her pants leg, but otherwise the uniform showed no other signs of injuries. "We now had proof of life for Jessica Lynch," Dupree would recall. Lori Piestawa's uniform, however, made it quite clear that she had already died from her wounds.

Back in Oklahoma at John Cain's home, his mother, Ruth, had been awake since 2 a.m. local time—from 11 a.m. on in An-Nasiriyah. Ruth had been fasting and praying daily for her son and for 2/8, but this time the Holy Spirit within her was really on fire. The intensity continued to build as she prayed. A little while later she called her daughters Jennifer and Rebecca, and they prayed together over the phone in a three-way teleconference. "We were driven to prayers. We just could not stop praying," Ruth recalled later. Ruth regularly prayed every morning at 6:00 local time, asking for the protection of Jesus' blood, calling on God to send His angels to protect 2/8, asking God to give the Marines unbelievable energy and alertness to see the things they needed to see. But this day was different. "There was a whole different level of energy. It was the most rigorous time of my life in prayer. It was the Lord!" she stated later.

The three Cain women ended up praying together over the phone several times that morning, until after 9 a.m. local time, or 6 p.m. in Iraq. Unknown to them, God had been leading them to pray right through the time of Fox Company's assault on the hospital. Over the next day as the news in America continually broadcast and analyzed the events of Jessica Lynch's capture, Ruth sensed that somehow their intense prayers on the 25th were related to the situation. Only months later did Ruth learn the full timing of events, how everything involving their prayers and the action in An-Nasiriyah clicked together.

Throughout the day of the 25th, as the First Marines advanced and Fox Company assaulted the hospital, Golf Company's Second Platoon was engaged with irregular Iraqi forces west of Highway 7. It was tough house-to-house urban warfare, just as David had believed he would be seeing. All day long the Iraqi irregulars were ducking in and out of trees and buildings, firing at Second Platoon and MacCutcheon's CAAT platoon that had moved north to support them. Sniper fire, mostly from the eastern hospital, was also being directed at them.

However, since their crushing in the firefights of the day before, many of the Fedayeen were no longer putting up much resistance during the house-to-house actions. Some were trying to hide or run away, and Second Platoon was beginning to capture significant numbers of EPWs. The battalion was beginning to see evidence of God's answering prayers to cause a spirit of fear and confusion to come upon the enemy.

Golf's First Platoon patrolling up north near the hospital was also engaged with Iraqi forces, heavily at times, again with much of the fire coming from the hospital. Miraculously, Golf Company did not incur a single casualty on the 25th. Late in the day, elements from Third Battalion, Second Marines moved up on 2/8's left flank, clearing and taking positions west of Highway 7. This enabled Second Platoon to disengage and return to Golf's defensive perimeter east of the highway.

The other maneuver elements of 2/8 also saw continuing engagements throughout the 25th. One noteworthy exchange involved MacCutcheon's CAAT platoon. One of MacCutcheon's primary responsibilities was to patrol and keep the major highways clear within 2/8's sector. His platoon engaged enemy forces every day from the 23rd through the 27th. On the 25th, an Iraqi D30 artillery battery—composed of Russian-made 122 mm towed howitzers—had engaged the CAAT platoon down south near the intersection of highways 7 and 8. MacCutcheon called for indirect artillery fire, which TAC approved. Starnes' 155 mm guns destroyed the Iraqi D30s. Despite heavy fire from the D30s, not a single vehicle or Marine from the CAAT platoon was hit that day. Referring to that strategic intersection of primary roads, Mortenson would later recall that "the contact down in that area was very regular."

Throughout the first three days in An-Nasiriyah, David's spirit and thoughts were uneasy every time he saw young, clean-shaven

Iraqi "civilians" walking south down Highway 7. The rules of engagement allowed 2/8 Marines to stop civilians they considered to be a potential threat, but it is the tactical situation and the judgment of the company officers and sergeants that make the immediate determination between potential threats and true civilians fleeing the fighting. During the first two days, Ross's men stopped several civilians heading south but found no Iraqi soldiers or Fedayeen.

But by the 25th, the situation was changing. It was obvious that more young Iraqi men were in the mix of civilians heading south. David was sensing foul play. They had fought and captured enough Iraqi soldiers and irregular Fedayeen, the latter always fighting in civilian clothing, to know what Iraqi military men looked like. The common civilians were largely poor, often unshaven and dressed in dirty or ragged clothing. The Fedayeen looked presentable, with clean haircuts and good clothes—and they often sported some attitude. There now was a fairly steady stream of "clean-cuts" casually walking down Highway 7 past Golf's defensive position.

David made a request of Sgt. Campbell: "Sarge, I've got a bad sense about these guys. Requesting permission to stop them and haul them in for questioning." Campbell replied, "If they're heading south they're no threat to us, so let them keep on moving." Golf had set up a machine-gun position at the south end of its sector to prevent anyone from doubling back into their section of the city, and so Campbell was content for the time being. But within a couple of days, David's conviction would be proved true. For now, however, he had to be patient and stay alert.

By the time evening came on the 25th, the sandstorms had stopped. The prayers of God's people were being answered. In addition to the storm having provided cover for Fox Company's assault, it had no negative impact on Task Force Tarawa and 2/8. Dupree would state later, "The sandstorms were not a negative factor. They had no negative influence on 2/8 operations." The weather then took a significantly different turn.

Overnight and into the early morning of Wednesday the 26th, rain poured down. It would be the only time this happened during

2/8's stay in Iraq. The rainfall was torrential. The Marines' fighting holes filled with water. The infantrymen got soaked, and the overnight temperature was relatively cold, around 50 degrees Fahrenheit. But another answer to prayer took place. "Between crossing the stream on March 24, the heavy rains the night of the 25th, and the continuous action for the rest of the war, I was really very surprised that none of 2/8 and Golf Marines suffered any trench foot or immersion-foot problems," Capt. Ross stated later. "Nobody developed blisters; we had no Marines go down for feet problems," he recalled.

The torrential rains also softened hard sandy ground and turned sun-baked hard turf into muddy fields that would remain wet and soft for the next few days. While the rains might have seemed a nuisance to the Marines at first, they would soon prove to be another timely and protective provision by God for 2/8.

Late in the day of the 25th, after clearing the hospital and destroying the captured weapons, Mortenson ordered Fox Company to withdraw to a new defensive position west of the hospital. The battalion had remained in contact with the enemy throughout the day—Echo Company was still exchanging fire with Iraqi positions west and north of the Euphrates River bridge and continued to receive sporadic sniper fire and occasional indirect fire from RPGs and mortars. To tighten Fox and Golf Company lines on his eastern position in case the fighting heated up to his west, Mortenson reduced the battalion's eastern perimeter a bit and vacated the hospital. The new position for Fox Company was near the perimeter of the hospital grounds, extended east by 200 meters from Fox's positions the night before. Mortenson also assigned a scout-sniper team to cover the hospital entrance from the north and east, to watch for any Iraqi attempt to re-enter the facility.

Fox's consolidated yet extended position from the previous night yielded a nice find. Sgt. Wolfe of the Scout-Sniper Platoon found small boats hidden in the weeds along the Euphrates River at the north end of Fox's new position. Dremann and Gatewood had been wondering how the Iraqi's had been bringing soldiers into the hospital, because 2/8 had all the highways and side roads covered. The Iraqis had been using the boats to ferry men across the river at night. The scout-snipers methodically destroyed the boats using thermite grenades.

Now keen to the Iraqis' use of boats, Mortenson ordered his sniper teams from that time forward to shoot any incoming Iraqi boats with .50-caliber sniper rounds, six inches below the water-line. The well-placed shots caused all boats attempting passage to sink. "We made the Iraqis swim back," Mortenson later explained. "We weren't sure at this point if they were friendly or foe, so we just sunk the boats." But Iraqi intentions regarding the hospital continued. Later that night the scout-sniper team spotted a squad of approximately ten Iraqi soldiers in tactical formation re-enter-ing the hospital amidst the rain. After holding discussions back at TAC, Mortenson decided he'd had enough of the Iraqi shenani-gans. He ordered an artillery barrage for the following morning.

The downpours stopped early in the morning of the 26th, and TAC called in the barrage from 1/10. "I fired my whole allot-ment of concrete-piercing shells into that hospital," Mortenson said later. "I wanted to kill the Iraqis that were trying to kill my Marines. We pounded the dog snot out of that hospital." It was quite a show. The accuracy of 1/10's fire was pinpoint. Upon securing the hospital the day before, Dremann had logged the hospital GPS grid coordinates into his hand-held GPS unit. With ten-digit accuracy to the GPS grid, 1/10 was able to fire in Mortenson's words "one-round, one-hit accuracy." That meant every round from 1/10 landed on target. Despite Fox and Golf Company Marines being close to the target, no friendly casual-ties occurred. The danger zone for 155 mm artillery is 400 meters, and elements of Golf Company were less than 500 meters away, while the eastern line of Fox was no more than 250 meters away. The incoming artillery attack was, in military jargon, "danger close." As Ross said, "We hunkered down, but it was impressive seeing the artillery coming in overhead."

Golf's Second Platoon was already clearing some homes and buildings west of Highway 7 when the barrage started around 9 a.m. "We could see the hospital crumbling during breaks in our actions," David said. "A lot of smoke and haze like a fireworks display." The whole southern half of the hospital was destroyed.

Fox Company then cleared and secured the hospital without a fight and found no survivors among the Iraqi squad that had re-entered the night before. The fight over the hospital had ended. It was such a hard-fought victory that Commanding General Natonski of Task Force Tarawa came in for a visit, and Kerry Sanders filed a live report from the scene.

The excitement on the 26th wasn't over yet for Golf Company. In the afternoon, two large artillery shells landed just south of Second Platoon, within about fifteen feet of several Marines. The shells didn't explode. "They should have gone off and killed quite a few Marines," Ross recalled. "They were apparently improperly fused. If they were U.S. artillery rounds, they are never duds, and it was by God's grace that they didn't explode."

Fulford later stated, "This event was replicated numerous times throughout the combat in An-Nasiriyah." Given the number of times that incoming artillery and mortar rounds failed to detonate during the conflict, no amount of argument could lead seasoned veterans like Fulford and Ross to think otherwise. Their unanimous conclusion was that God was protecting them.

The battle for An-Nasiriyah was now well into day four, and the combined Iraqi Army Eleventh Infantry Division and Fedayeen forces had been mauled by Task Force Tarawa. "For three days the Iraqis hooked and jabbed with 1/2 and 2/8, and we kicked the dog snot out of them every time they did anything," Mortenson said later. "They threw themselves against two infantry battalions and got their butts handed to them." Miraculously, 2/8 had suffered only ten wounded. But the most eventful fight of the whole war for 2/8 was about to take place, and God would once again see them through.

7

THE NIGHT OF MARCH 26

The angel of the LORD encamps all around those who fear Him, and delivers them.

—PSALM 34:7

He shall call upon Me, and I will answer him; I will be with him in trouble; I will deliver him and honor him.

—PSALM 91:15

...there is the certainty that their sense of duty and honor will be strengthened by the assurance that every Marine is, first and foremost, a rifleman.

—FROM *LEADING MARINES*

A S NIGHT CAME ON MARCH 25, Mortenson and Fulford sat down to talk about their tactical situation. Discussing the lack of success of the Iraqi attacks, Mortenson told Fulford, "These guys are going to get tired of throwing themselves against 2/8. I think they're going to get smart, walk another 4,000 meters south and attack our soft targets." This referred to the logistics of H&S Company and the Main situated along Highway 8, south of Golf Company's defensive perimeter. Fulford agreed. Mortenson and Fulford then planned to move Main and their log train north the next day and have protective berms and bunkers constructed around their new position.

On the morning of March 26 Mortenson drove to RCT-2

headquarters and met with Colonel Bailey to review his assessment and plan for moving 2/8's Main and log train and bunkering them in. Mortenson also suggested to Bailey that he organize his logistical units in a more force-protective position. Bailey concurred with the plan, and Mortenson called Maj. Alford down in the Main and told him to move his units 3,000 meters north toward the rifle companies. "I thought it would be far enough," Mortenson recalled. "They were about 1,000 meters south and had their own organic security, so they weren't going to get overrun."

Alford completed the movement that morning, setting up a new base around some abandoned gas station buildings just west of Highway 8, about 1,000 meters south of Golf Company and south of the intersection of Highway 7 and Highway 8. A railroad track running east to west and parallel to Highway 8 was positioned between their new location and Highway 8 to the north, and swampy marshes lay on both sides of the railroad track. There was a high bridge overpass on Highway 8 over the railroad track. A complex of industrial buildings straddled Highway 8 north of the new position of Main's and 2/8's log train and west of Highway 7. The Fedayeen had been using some of these buildings for cover to fire on 2/8 over the last three days, and elements of Golf and Echo had previously cleared part of the complex.

As CO of H&S Company, Capt. Ryans went about the work of setting up the perimeter defense, placing machine guns, rocket and grenade launchers, and instructing his men in their areas of cover responsibility. Alford called in armored combat earthmovers, or "ACEs"—armored bulldozers in layman's terms—from Company A of the Second Combat Engineering battalion to create protective berms in a rectangular perimeter around their position. The location selected by Alford provided an easily defended position that allowed both the Main and 2/8 log train to fit within a single berm configuration. In total there were about 120 Marines at Main and H&S, virtually all in supporting roles including logistics, administration, mechanics, communications, and medical corpsmen along with some combat engineers.

Back in western New York, around 7:20 a.m. and 3:20 p.m.

Iraqi time, I was in the midst of praying our now standard list of petitions before the Lord when the Holy Spirit quickened me to turn to Psalm 34. Verse 7 really stood out: "The angel of the Lord encamps all around those who fear Him, and delivers them." I prayed this verse for David and all of 2/8, and then left for work. Only after the events about to unfold for Main and H&S did the reason become clear why God had me and surely many other believers pray this specific prayer.

Back in An-Nasiriyah, Mortenson was engaging his rifle companies in house-to-house sweeps throughout much of the day of the 26th, and he had begun rotating their defensive positions to keep any remaining Iraqis in the vicinity off balance. To maintain control of the Euphrates River bridge, he created Task Force Mohawk, which consisted of approximately 70 men pulled together from a mix of 2/8 units—including a Light Armored Reconnaissance (LAR) platoon, some scout-snipers, and a heavy machine-gun CAAT section. Mortenson placed Capt. Ryans in charge of the task force. Ryans and Task Force Mohawk spent the afternoon at the bridge as part of the northern-most unit in the battalion. For Ryans, his new assignment got him a little excited. "Lt. Col. Mortenson had given me what I thought I wanted," he said later.

The day of March 26 also saw a major artillery barrage from 1/10 onto suspected Iraqi positions west of 2/8 and 3/2 sectors. The Iraqis were reported to be massing for a counter-attack around a train station located further west into An-Nasiriyah along the railroad and Highway 8, running east to west and situated north of 2/8's Main and log train positions. Starnes' battalion fired a "full battalion ten," meaning all eighteen of 1/10's 155 mm field guns each fired ten rounds on target for a total barrage of 180 artillery rounds.

The barrage could be heard throughout the afternoon by 2/8 Marines, who understood from the sound and shaking of the ground that a major bombardment was underway. It was evident to 2/8's TAC and Main that such a large bombardment would decimate much if not all of any massing enemy force. Still, there was a real possibility of elements of Iraqi units slipping away from

117

the attack and re-forming to strike. And Mortenson, Alford, and Fulford were pretty sure that Main and the 2/8 log train would be the intended target of any Iraqi attack.

To further strengthen the firepower available for Alford, Lt. Col. Dunahoe of 3/2 had loaned Mortenson a section of his CAAT platoon. Mortenson deployed this added section along with MacCutcheon and two of his platoon sections south around the intersection of Highways 7 and 8 near the railroad overpass. This provided a total of twelve CAAT Humvees close to Alford and Main. Later Yeo recalled the apprehension of the situation: "We had intel that we were supposed to anticipate an Iraqi counterattack that night. Everyone was very tense."

Down at the southern end of 2/8's sector, late in the afternoon, a platoon of combat engineers had been patrolling northwest of Main's position and had found an Iraqi ammunition cache near the railroad, which they proceeded to blow up. It had just gotten dark, around 8 p.m., as the combat engineers were walking back to Main. Undetected by 2/8, at least two groups of Fedayeen had been slipping their way east, one group walking near the railroad northwest of Main, the second near the swamp north of Main. Likely surprised by the new location of Main, seeing the combat engineers returning and with MacCutcheon's CAAT sections and the ACE bulldozers and other vehicles sitting to their north along Highway 8, the Fedayeen began shooting.

It is not known whether this was a carefully planned attack, or whether these Iraqi forces were simply remnants from 1/10's barrage earlier in the day. Dupree believed the Iraqis had been making their way back to the cache site to restock with ammunition, and opened up when they saw the Marines now behind and in front of them. But almost certainly they were knowingly targeting Main and 2/8's log train.

At first the Fedayeen fired AK-47s and machine guns with their distinctive green tracers, but soon added RPGs and small-mortar fire. Inside the Main perimeter, Marines threw on their helmets, and machine gunners opened up, firing back, with red tracers slicing the darkness. Alford was in the Main CP tent with some of his staff officers, including 1st Lt. Chad Ragan. As incoming bullets began ripping through their tent, Alford reacted as coolly as his Marines had come to expect. Later Ragan would recall, "I will never forget what Alford said as the rounds started coming in. He said in his drawl, 'Boys, grab your long guns and get out there and fight!'" The officers carry 9 mm pistols, but the image Alford had just expressed of bygone soldiers fetching muskets or flintlock rifles was taken to heart.

His officers and staff quickly dispersed into the compound to help direct the fight. Alford then grabbed an M-16 and joined the fray, stepping out of the tent and firing at a source of green tracers. The shooting quickly escalated into a heavy firefight. Alford ordered everyone to the perimeter berms, while he stayed in the center of the compound at a gas station building trying to maintain a good view of the battlefield in front of him.

Unable to locate a radio within the Main tent, Alford walked about thirty feet to a nearby Humvee parked in the open that carried his mobile high-power field radio. The Marines instruct their men never to sleep in a vehicle and always to dismount from nonarmored vehicles when under fire, because the enemy will target vehicles during an attack. But for Alford there was no other way to direct his men's fighting. He needed the radio to maintain contact with Mortenson and Fulford in the TAC CP up north, and by standing at the Humvee in the open he made himself a likely target. Focused and courageous, he remained at the Humvee for the duration of the fight despite numerous enemy rounds whizzing by.

As the fight intensified, two Humvees from the Second Combat Engineering platoon were hit by RPGs, destroying them and sending shrapnel and flames in every direction. But the 2/8 Marines reacted in heroic fashion. One such Marine was Lcpl. McDonald. He was blown off his roof position along with the body of his machine gun, but miraculously landed unhurt. Because his ammunition and gun barrel were still on the roof, he climbed back up as bullets and tracers shot by and retrieved his ammo and barrel. He then reassembled his weapon and got back into the battle.

The Fedayeen had also started firing at the ACEs and CAAT Humvees sitting north and east of them on Highway 8. MacCutcheon's CAAT platoon was situated by the intersection with

Highway 7, near the railroad overpass. David's buddy John Cain was sitting in the lead Humvee of MacCutcheon's CAAT section Gold. "A RPG round landed near Capt. MacCutcheon's Humvee, and I could see the green tracer fire bouncing off the ACEs. Nothing was damaged," Cain said later.

Because of the frequent clashes of the last four days around the intersection of Highways 7 and 8 and within the industrial park along Highway 8 to the immediate west, RCT-2 headquarters was paying a lot of attention to the escalating battle. The HQ was located just south of 2/8's Main, and Iraqi bullets had started cutting into Colonel Bailey's command tent, sending everyone sprawling for cover. He was not in any mood to underestimate the Iraqis.

Bailey ordered 1/10 to fire a battalion six—108 rounds of artillery—into the industrial area. The bombardment created large chunks of shrapnel, some of which flew across Highway 8 as well as Highway 7. Miraculously, no shrapnel hit any of MacCutcheon's CAAT vehicles, but there were some near misses. "I saw chunks of shrapnel curve to miss our vehicles," Cain would recall. "I saw one chunk heading straight for me—then almost like someone pushed on it, it was driven into the ground. No doubt the Lord was protecting us!"

MacCutcheon then moved his platoon up to higher ground to the railroad overpass south on Highway 8, to enable his Humvees to better engage the Iraqis, firing to the west and southwest. Fortunately MacCutcheon was in continuous radio contact with Mortenson and TAC throughout the firefight. Quickly getting a good grasp of the extent of the Iraqi attack due to Alford's and MacCutcheon's input, Mortenson called Bailey at RCT-2 headquarters and requested a LAR platoon for fire support. Bailey approved, and sent Capt. Grunwald's unit, which was positioned north by the Saddam Canal with First Battalion-Second Marines. LAR units are equipped with LAVs—with their deadly 25 mm guns—which was the reason Mortenson specifically requested them. "I wanted the LAVs to sweep out there because the Iraqis were terrified of the LAVs. I knew once the LAVs got into the attack down there and started supporting Dale, it would break up the attack," Mortenson would later state.

To help ensure he had overwhelming firepower, Mortenson also requested and received approval to bring a section of two M1A1 Abrams battle tanks down from 1/2's sector to support Alford. Capt. Grunwald's platoon began their move south, through ambush alley, crossed the Euphrates River bridge, and drove through 2/8's sector, past Fox Company, Mortenson and crew in the TAC, and past Golf Company. In radio contact with Grunwald the whole time, Mortenson instructed him that MacCutcheon and his CAAT section were waiting at the railroad overpass and would link up with him to get him oriented after Grunwald arrived with his LAVs. "I didn't want those LAVs just driving down there shooting [expletive]," Mortenson recalled later. It took the LAR platoon about twenty minutes after the order came in from Bailey to transit the few miles from 1/2 down to MacCutcheon.

While Grunwald's LAVs were moving south, the firefight raged around Main and H&S Company. Alford requested 81 mm mortar fire on the Fedayeen positions, which were close to his own perimeter. He had memorized the GPS coordinates of the four corners of his perimeter berm defenses, and he radioed TAC to fire onto an area 300 meters further northwest of the northwest corner of his perimeter. "I still remember those GPS coordinates," Alford would say months later while being interviewed. "That northwest corner was grid point 200304. I was using it as a reference, telling Weapons Company to land them out beyond that point where the Fedayeen were firing from."

Alford kept hearing another Marine inside the perimeter berm yelling on the radio, also trying to tell TAC CP where to shoot. The Marine was using one of the grid coordinate cards that Luciano had passed out days before. Alford yelled into the radio, "Hey stud, who is this calling for fire? This is Alford." The Marine turned out to be Cpl. Heath, a young man Alford had recruited back in the late 1990s when he was in charge of the Nashville, Tennessee, Marines' recruiting district. "Forget all that card stuff!" Alford yelled at Heath. "I'm calling out the GPS positions—you just tell me what you see falling!" Alford effectively turned Heath into his forward observer. After a correction or two, 2/8's mortars started landing right on target.

Under the cover of the berm, Chaplain Rogers found himself hugging the ground next to a few Marines. Recognizing Rogers, a sergeant yelled over the noise of the battle. "Sir, we'd really appreciate it if you'd pray out loud!" Rogers started shouting prayers. "Lord, keep us safe; Lord, keep us focused, help us defeat our enemy; Lord, don't let the Iraqis shoot straight!"

At the time the firefight started, Ryans was up north driving south on Highway 7 with a reserve platoon to join up with one of the CAAT sections when he saw the battle unfolding. His first thoughts were: *These are my men. I'm supposed to be with my men!* Unable to reach his company in time to help, he realized he had only one option. "I was put in a position where all I could do was pray for my Marines," Ryans said later. "I just sat there, saying at first, 'Lord, protect them.' Then I could visually see in my mind the defenses I had set up that morning, where I had placed machine guns, and the like. As I listened in on the radio, I could figure out: OK, these guys are right here. I could visualize where everybody was and piece it all together. I prayed for each guy there, knowing exactly where they were."

Of all the 2/8 Marines, Ryans—with his thorough knowledge of his men and the fortifications—was the exact person one would want calling on the Lord in prayer during this fight. God had just the right believer in just the right position calling on Him to move His Hand supernaturally to protect the Marines in Main and H&S Company.

With the intensity of the fight undiminished, Alford called TAC to request artillery fire onto the Fedayeen positions. Since most of the Fedayeen positions were less than 400 meters from the berm positions, all incoming artillery fire from 1/10 would be danger close. Within minutes of Alford's request, 155 mm rounds from 1/10 started landing on target. At least three separate artillery missions in support of Alford and Main were called during the fight by Mortenson in TAC.

One of the effects from the torrential rains of the night before was muddy, soft ground. An unexpected benefit of the mud was becoming apparent to the Marines within Main's defensive position. The incoming Iraqi mortar rounds were landing, but instead of exploding immediately upon contact and sending their deadly shrapnel out above the ground, they were sinking about six inches into the soft, muddy ground and detonating below the surface. Much of the blasts from the mortar explosions were being absorbed by the surrounding mud, resulting in a significantly reduced amount of shrapnel flying out toward the Marines. And because the mud was absorbing the expanding part of the explosions, most of the blast effects that did break the surface exploded straight up. The previous night's rain shower, miserable though it had been for the 2/8 Marines, was providentially being used this night to protect them from death and injury.

The fight had been raging for approximately thirty minutes when Grunwald's LAR platoon met up with MacCutcheon's CAAT section Gold near the railroad overpass on Highway 8. Grunwald, who had been in radio contact with Mortenson the whole time of his transit, acknowledged to Mortenson that he had linked up with MacCutcheon. MacCutcheon then spent a few minutes orienting Grunwald to the battlefield situation, identifying the location of the engaged Iraqi units and the location of Alford, Main, and H&S.

Mortenson then spoke with Grunwald to define the area of his LAV attack, telling him to sweep east to west and keep the effects of all his fire north of the 3-1 grid line. The 3-1 grid line was 1,400 meters north of Main, a sufficient distance to keep Grunwald's platoon from shooting up Main and 2/8's log train. Grunwald then positioned his platoon on the overpass, looking down on the battlefield, and began to systematically sweep his fire east to west as planned, with devastating effect.

From their superior firing position, Grunwald's LAR platoon continued to light up Iraqi positions for several minutes. About forty-five minutes into the fight and ten minutes or so after the LAVs started shooting, the easternmost LAV—situated on Grunwald's left flank—became disoriented. The dangerous element of friendly fire suddenly was added to the already violent firefight between 2/8 and the Fedayeen. The disoriented LAV mistakenly began firing its 25 mm cannon at the seven-ton trucks of H&S sitting inside the defensive perimeter. The fire was extraordinarily destructive. The LAV targeted the closest truck, set it ablaze, and systematically began hitting the next truck in line. Seeing the trucks being set off, Chaplain Rogers knew something was wrong. *This can't be the Iraqis shooting*, he thought. *They're not that good!*

Mortenson, Alford, and Fulford also took notice. The accuracy and crescendo of the incoming fire caused a sudden increase in casualties, which was being reported over the radios. The events of the fight had started to go bad very quickly. Mortenson later explained, "[It seemed] that all of a sudden, the Iraqis got real good, real fast. At this point Alford had a couple of casualties, but all of a sudden it increased incrementally when that 25 mm gun started hitting.... All of a sudden he's getting casualties and things were blowing up." They too began to suspect that there might be a "blue on blue"—a friendly fire situation in progress—but there was too much fighting still going on for them to discern the situation clearly.

Other Marines now rose to the occasion. Three trucks had been hit and were on fire. A fourth truck not yet hit was full of ammunition and was a sitting duck. If it went up, dozens of Marines would be killed. Gunny Sergeant Walker of H&S yelled to Pfc. Smith, the closest Marine to the ammo truck. "Jump in that ammo truck and move it out of here!" Walker ordered. The ammo truck was parked amid three other trucks—two were on the driver's side; the other on the passenger side. All three were burning. Flames on the driver's side were too close and too intense for Smith to get in that way, so he ran to the passenger side, dodging lesser flames there and jumped in the cab. With shooting ongoing, he backed the ammo truck around behind the gas station building near where Alford was, taking the truck out of the LAV line of fire. For his heroism, Smith was awarded the Bronze Star.

With the battle intensity undiminished, and with H&S trucks burning, MacCutcheon called TAC to request a close air-support attack. MacCutcheon had identified Iraqi vehicles shooting at his CAAT platoon from the west and southwest; later he stated they were Iraqi ZSU vehicles and pickup trucks carrying Fedayeen. The ZSUs were a real cause for concern. Russian-designed, the

ZSUs are self-propelled vehicles that carry cannons capable of attacking both ground targets and low-flying aircraft. Marine AV-8 Harriers were stacked over the battlefield in Close Air Support (CAS) formation, circling at 10,000 feet and itching to drop their ordnance on an approved target. Up in TAC, Mortenson, Fulford, Luciano, and the fire-support-cell air officer reviewed Mac-Cutcheon's request and concluded the geometry of the Harrier attack mission was unsafe. Any approach by the Harriers would require them to drop ordnance far too close to 2/8 Marines to be reasonably sure of avoiding friendly casualties. TAC denied the mission. Chaplain Rogers would later state, "The AV-8's probably would have killed us if they had dropped their stuff."

Shortly after the Harriers were called off, and with Main and H&S continuing to receive hits from both the wayward LAV and the Iraqis, Alford requested an immediate suppression fire from 1/10 artillery, extremely danger close at only 50 meters beyond his northern berm positions. Luciano didn't want to fire the mission, believing it was too close to Main's position. Mortenson immediately got on the radio with Alford to ask him personally about his request. Alford told him, "I need it," to which Mortenson replied, "Get 'em down because here it comes." Mortenson then called into the regimental TAC-NET and talked directly to his old friend Glenn Starnes to clear the request with him. Starnes then three times fired a "battery three," meaning the six guns of a battery unit within 1/10 each fired three rounds three times for a total of 54 artillery rounds, all to land within 50 meters of Main's northern berm.

The incoming rounds silenced the remaining Iraqis. Fortunately, another miracle of protection occurred during 1/10's barrage. Of the 54 rounds of 155 mm artillery fired, two rounds landed slightly off target and within Main's defensive perimeter, which normally would have killed several Marines. However, God continued to protect 2/8. The first round slammed into the ground but was a dud. The second round hit the top of a concrete overhang on the gas station, just 30 feet from where Alford was standing by his Humvee. The explosion detonated on the overhang, and as a result it exploded upward and outward from that high point. Despite being within the 100 percent-kill radius of the 155 mm round, Alford in effect was underneath the blast and shielded from the explosion. Miraculously, he was unhurt. Had that incoming round landed only one or two feet from where it did, it would have missed the overhang and hit the ground. The resulting explosion at ground level would have killed Alford. God was providing miraculous protection for Main and H&S.

With the Iraqis out of the fight, now only the one wayward LAV continued to shoot at Main and H&S. Right around this time an RCT-2 fire-control officer noticed that the position coordinates identified by Grunwald's LAR platoon for incoming fire were very close to the artillery fire coordinates being requested by 2/8. The disoriented LAV was reporting its position as receiving indirect fire, because the vehicle had been drifting south and was close to the area of incoming 1/10 artillery and 2/8's 81 mm fire. RCT-2 headquarters immediately requested 2/8's TAC CP to de-conflict the situation. Alford then requested, and Mortenson approved, a fire mission to illuminate the battlefield and ordered the 81 mm mortars from 2/8's Weapons Company to fire illumination rounds, or "starbursts," into the sky.

Grunwald immediately radioed in and acknowledged the situation, stating "I've got illumination over me." Mortenson and Alford then quickly concluded that an LAV from Grunwald's LAR platoon was shooting at them. A few minutes later a cease-fire was achieved. The battle had lasted close to ninety minutes, with friendly fire from the one disoriented LAV creating most of the damage in Main and H&S during the latter half of the fight.

Alford and his men immediately started assessing their casualties. Up north in TAC, grim faces awaited Alford's report. "This was the toughest time during the whole war," Dupree would recall. "That was the time, the waiting, when we really had the lump in our throats, as it took some time to gather the information." Fulford later stated, "We certainly feared the worst, thought we could have twenty or thirty dead." But he wasn't going to idly sit by and let fear get the best of him. Fulford called TAC's Marines to prayer. As the men gathered in a circle and prayed, each one asked God for His intervention and favor, for no Marine in Main to die, for God to spare all who had been injured. Dupree added another request, asking God for strength to get through this. Sitting in his Humvee on Highway 7, Ryans also called on the Lord to miraculously spare his injured Marines.

The reports from Alford then started coming in. A total of thirty-one Marines from 2/8 had been wounded. Most had shrapnel wounds. A few of the wounded had been hit by bullets, but none had been killed. Several of the wounded were injured seriously enough that the Navy corpsmen had to use the new QuicKlot bandages to stop their bleeding. Medical reports later confirmed that these QuicKlot bandages saved the lives of at least seven of the wounded 2/8 Marines. Mortenson later stated, "The seven lives were saved by great medical attention, great medical gear, and the intervention of the Almighty."

Considering the duration and intensity of the fight, the results were simply miraculous. Alford called for an evacuation of the wounded to the regimental field hospital to ensure his men would receive the most intensive medical care as quickly as possible. While awaiting the medevac vehicles, Chaplain Rogers and 1st Lt. T.J. Owens—XO of H&S Company and also a believer in Jesus Christ—prayed together over each of the wounded. They also prayed with every uninjured Marine who requested prayer.

Understandably, emotions were running high in many. One young Marine, Lcpl. Brass, had tears in his eyes as he prayed with Chaplain Rogers and Owens. He had taken a 7.62 mm AK-47 round to his chest, but the SAPI plate in his flak jacket stopped the round, saving his life. The SAPI plate, for "small arms protective insert," was designed for shrapnel and pistol rounds, but stopping a high-powered rifle round is not guaranteed. God answered the prayers of His people that night. All of the thirty-one wounded stabilized in less than a day. A few of the wounded stayed with 2/8 in Iraq, but most were sent to an American military hospital in Germany and eventually back to the United States to recuperate. Some of the wounded required follow-up surgery. But all remained on active duty and none were discharged from the Corps for medical reasons. All thirty-one certainly were hurt in the battle, but none ultimately were harmed.

It also became apparent as Alford, Rogers, and Owens made their rounds that individual acts of heroism had been common. Gunny Haney, the senior sergeant from MacCutcheon's CAAT platoon, happened to be on site that night. He took several shrapnel wounds but kept fighting despite much bleeding. For his gallantry in combat, Gunny Haney was nominated for the Silver Star. Dedication to duty was evidently paramount with Haney. Sent to a Navy hospital in Kuwait to recover from his wounds, Haney quickly grew impatient. He managed to sneak out of the hospital and return to his CAAT platoon long before he would have been formally cleared to rejoin 2/8.

Navy Corpsman Alan Dementer was awarded a Bronze Star for heroic actions during the firefight for attending to six wounded Marines who were caught outside the protective berm. What made Dementer's actions so special was he had already been wounded by shrapnel in his right shoulder and knee before braving the fire and jumping over the berm to save the lives of the wounded Marines.

The evening firefight and the resulting casualties made the network news back in the United States the night of the 26th. Like the believers within 2/8 who prayed for God to mercifully spare their wounded, countless Christians across America also went to prayer. Some of them were dedicated believers of the Calvary Chapel of the Finger Lakes (CCFL), one of the largest churches in the western New York region. Senior pastor Bill Galatin had formed a continuous, 24/7 prayer effort when the war started on March 19 and continued the effort until major hostilities ended in mid-May. Every minute of every day during the two months of major combat, at least one believer and typically several at CCFL were in prayer at their church.

They would print out and post on their prayer board the names of the American servicemen and women who had become casualties—killed, wounded, and missing in action, or known to be prisoners of war—and would pray for them and their families. This night of March 26 was an especially intense time of prayer as the firefight and casualties of 2/8 were reported. The believers at CCFL continued to pray for the 2/8 wounded and families for the next few days. Undoubtedly, many churches across the country had a similar 24/7 prayer effort, and undoubtedly this enormous volume of prayers helped affect the will of the Lord in sparing the wounded of 2/8.

Evidently God responded to the prayers for the American POWs as well. Later in the war Marines rescued all the missing American POWs in Tikrit, north of Baghdad, including Shoshana Johnson and her fellow soldiers from the Army's 507th Maintenance Company. Not one American serviceman or woman would remain MIA by the conclusion of the major fighting against Hussein's forces.

Looking back on the fight, the men of 2/8 had one common conclusion: God had protected them once again. Alford would say, "It was a miracle from God that the 25 mm LAV gun didn't cut one of my Marines in half!" Ragan would later state, "There is no explanation for that night, except divine intervention. There's no two ways about it. The Lord watched over us." Fulford was still moved several months after the incident while being interviewed. "There were 31 casualties that night," he said. "There were some flat-out miracles that occurred.... Personally, there is no question in my mind that the Lord's hand was upon us." Mortenson was succinct. "Thank God nobody was killed!" he later said, then added, "We were truly blessed by the fact that nobody was whacked dead!" And Ryans had a revelation from it all. "As the reports came in, and nobody had died, my prayers became praise: 'Thank you, Lord, nobody died!' It turned my fear into praising God! It helped me in praising God. That's how the heaviness was lifted."

As was the case throughout the war, the Marines had also helped themselves considerably in the outcome through their preparation, training, and technology. "It was very helpful that we built and finished the berms earlier in the day," Alford recalled. Chaplain Rogers added, "The three weeks of Marine Combat Training that every Marine gets really paid off." Mortenson later emphasized that H&S Company underwent the same intensive training and deployments as the rest of the battalion, which resulted in excellent unit cohesiveness. Immediately after the cease-fire was achieved, Navy corpsmen Paul Johnson, Alan Dementer, and others did a terrific job treating the wounded. And the advanced technology of the QuicKlot bandages saved lives. Ragan later gave a lot of credit to Alford, as well, stating, "Alford saved 120 lives that night, the way he acted." Simply put, the Marines and corpsmen did their part exceedingly well, and God did the rest.

The effect on 2/8 operations from the destruction of the supply trucks was insignificant. The destroyed trucks mostly carried MREs, the battlefield "Meals Ready to Eat." Other than the men receiving only one MRE instead of the normal three over the next twenty-four hours, there was no adverse effect. At the end of four days of heavy fighting, every Iraqi attack on 2/8 had been crushed. The control of Highway 7 and the adjacent areas of the city were solidly in the grip of RCT-2. There would be about a week more of fighting in An-Nasiriyah, but the battles had devastated the Iraqi resistance. Miraculously, 2/8 had suffered only forty wounded, none dead, and none missing in action. And miracles of protection and favor were to continue. After the March 26 evening firefight until 2/8 left Iraq in May, the unit would take no more casualties. The heaviest fighting was over. From that time forward the Marines of 2/8 and Task Force Tarawa would turn their part of the war into a rout.

8

Sealing Victory in An-Nasiriyah

I will be glad and rejoice in Your mercy, for You have considered my trouble; you have known my soul in adversities, and have not shut me up into the hand of the enemy.

—Psalm 31:7-8

Creating and sustaining superior fighting power requires the combination of the tangible activities of war—maneuver, firepower, and protection—with the intangible elements of war—leadership, unit esprit, and individual courage.

—from *Leading Marines*

T HE MORNING OF MARCH 27 started off with a quiet calm. Chaplain Rogers had decided to put more emphasis into one-on-one ministry with 2/8 Marines. "I started a fire-hole-to-fire-hole ministry," he said. He headed north to Echo Company with Seaman Matthew Staszak, his religious programmer aide and sometime bodyguard. Making contact first with Capt. Yeo, the three met up with 1st Sgt. Hawkins and proceeded to visit Echo Marines in their fighting positions. As Chaplain Rogers prayed with a couple of Marines at their fighting hole, a RPG round landed about 10 feet from them. It was a dud.

East and south of Echo, the men of Golf Company had just finished planning their morning patrols. Fox Company had already begun firing on Iraqi positions across the Euphrates River, and had called for 81 mm mortar fire from TAC CP. In one of only two or three targeting errors made throughout the war by Weapons Company, the target coordinates were improperly adjusted and the first few mortar rounds were launched toward the position of Second Platoon of Golf Company. David was standing about 15 feet away from several of his buddies and heard the incoming mortars in flight. *These sound like they're coming at us,* he thought, and instinctively hit the ground.

Looking to his right, past his buddies by about fifteen feet, he saw a mortar explode. His buddies were within the kill radius of the mortar, and David was well within the injury area, but miraculously not one of them was hit. In between them and the mortar round had stood an Iraqi farmer's emaciated cow. It took the full brunt of the explosion. "That cow was blown to bits," David recalled, "but not one piece of shrapnel got through to us." If that mortar round had landed closer to them or farther away than it did by one or two feet, shrapnel would have missed the cow and probably hit them. The mortar had landed in the precise position necessary for the explosion to be absorbed by the cow.

A second mortar round landed at almost the same instant a little farther away from David's squad. Standing a good distance away from the impact of the second mortar round, Lieutenant Fitzsimmons, Second Platoon's commander, nevertheless took a piece of shrapnel from it to his chest. The force of the shrapnel created a permanent crease in his SAPI plate but otherwise did no harm. Capt. Ross and 1st Sgt. Beith were sitting just south of Second Platoon's position, and Beith jumped on the radio and yelled for a cease-fire. Weapons company re-evaluated their target data and proceeded to fire correctly on the Iraqi positions.

Afterward, Ross was philosophical about the near accident. "The lethality of U.S. weapons systems are much greater than the enemy's, so on the occasional mistake we make in targeting, usually we inflict more damage to ourselves than the enemy ever could," he later said. For Luciano's Weapons Company and Starnes' 1/10, their work during the battle for An-Nasiriyah can only be considered superb. From March 23 until the battalion left An-Nasiriyah on April 3, a span of twelve days, 1/10 fired more than 600 artillery rounds into 2/8's sector, 2/8's Weapons Company fired more than 400 of their large 81 mm mortar rounds, and Luciano approved twenty-seven air strikes and did not inflict a single friendly fire casualty on 2/8. For his extraordinary leadership and execution as Weapons Company commander and fire support coordinator for 2/8, Capt. Luciano was awarded the Bronze Star. And God saw to it that the few misdirected rounds that did land within 2/8 positions during that time caused no harm.

For the previous four days, 2/8 had been fighting a mixture of Iraqi forces. Initially many of the Iraqis were units from the Eleventh Division who were reported in the ridiculously inaccurate propaganda broadcasts from Baghdad to be routing the invading infidels of America and Britain. As these Eleventh Division soldiers were whipped in combat by Task Force Tarawa early on, the Iraqi opposition quickly turned into irregular forces. "They donned civilian clothes and mingled with crowds," Mortenson described later. "They were morally reprehensible." Most of the irregulars were Fedayeen. The Fedayeen paramilitary militia was under the direction of Uday Hussein, Saddam's older son, and they effectively formed the bulk of the resistance in An-Nasiriyah.

Fulford described the difference between the regular Iraqi army and Fedayeen. "With the notable exception of some fanatical paramilitary guys [Fedayeen], the average Iraqi soldier would stay in position while he felt safe, and would then flee and try to blend into civilian folk when his life was in danger," he would recall. The Fedayeen always wore civilian clothes, and routinely attempted to use children and women as human shields. "They would at gunpoint commandeer cars with women and children in the front seat, with the irregular militia in the back seats carrying AK-47s," Mortenson said. "They would jump out in a town square, run and spray bullets over a fence where they thought we were."

It wasn't just the cowardly actions of the individual Fedayeen and Iraqi soldiers that the Marines found so reprehensible. It was also the constant use of civilian facilities—hospitals, schools, mosques—as hiding places to shoot from and as storage for weapons and ammunition caches, all clear violations of the Geneva Convention, that further angered the men of 2/8.

But the Marines as a fighting organization are well-equipped to handle such irregular tactics. With their legendary sniper teams embedded in their battalions, the Marines actively hunted down these paramilitary militia. In the lead up to the deployment of 2/8 to Iraq, Alford had recommended to Mortenson to consider increasing the normal Scout-Sniper Platoon complement from eighteen to twenty-four, to enable 2/8 to deploy six teams of four men each. Mortenson liked the idea, and he and Alford worked with 1st Lt. Gregory Nolan, the Scout-Sniper Platoon commander, to reach that goal.

"Over the prior year, we built it," Mortenson later explained. "It takes time to train those guys. You just don't snap your fingers and give them six new Marines and all of a sudden call them two more teams." Mortenson assigned a four-man team—two snipers and two spotters—to each Rifle Company, leaving three more such teams to be deployed as needed within the battalion sector. Nolan's augmented Scout-Sniper Platoon achieved great success in An-Nasiriyah.

Spotting Fedayeen in cars, trucks, and buildings, the 2/8 snipers picked them off at an impressive rate. Confident of their shooting skills, the snipers would even shoot Fedayeen right through car windows, turning their cowardly tactics of commandeering vehicles with mothers and children inside into a deadly gamble. The chief sniper of 2/8, Cpl. Vasquez, racked up fourteen confirmed kills in just eleven days of combat in An-Nasiriyah. The Scout-Sniper Platoon as a whole totaled thirty-eight confirmed kills over that time. For his exceptional performance, Vasquez was awarded the Bronze Star.

While the 2/8 sniper teams achieved great success over time, they couldn't prevent all Iraqi sniping, especially during the first several days in An-Nasiriyah. Over the first five days in the city, David and many rifle company Marines experienced fairly regular enemy sniper fire. "Two or three times a day I'd hear or see a bullet land close enough to make me think I was the intended target," David would recall. "But after March 28 or 29, their sniping pretty much stopped. Our guys were really bagging them." Not a single 2/8 Marine sustained a casualty from enemy sniper fire throughout the war, which is quite miraculous. With divine protection and deadly Marine sniper fire taking its toll, Iraqi snipers were rendered totally ineffective.

By March 27 in the battle for An-Nasiriyah both the Fedayeen and regular Iraqi soldiers were hardly fighting at all. As Golf Company swept and cleared houses and buildings on the 27th, they began to capture large numbers of EPWs. "The Fedayeen were no longer putting up any resistance during our house-to-house searches," David said. "They basically were trying to hide or escape dressed as civilians." Their clean-shaven look and better clothing gave them away.

The rifle companies all started finding Baath Party officials in addition to the regular soldiers and Fedayeen, along with lots of documents, intel, weapons, and ordnance. The documents and intel were sent up the chain of command. Any person found with a weapon was taken prisoner, and any head of a home who denied having weapons but later was found hiding them when searched was also taken prisoner.

During midday on the 27th, First Squad-Second Platoon of Golf Company made a chilling discovery. In the back courtyard of a home, Sgt. Campbell's squad came upon a detailed sand model of Golf's defensive position from their first three days in An-Nasiriyah. Every fighting hole, every machine gun and mortar placement was accurately located in this scale model. David's bad sense a few days earlier as he observed clean-cut Iraqi men walking south past their position had been correct. It was now clear to David that his sense had been in fact a warning from the Holy Spirit. Those clean-cuts hadn't been innocent civilians, they were Iraqi soldiers and Fedayeen scoping out Golf's position. Considering the accuracy of the model, it is even more amazing that Golf had made it through the fight unscathed.

Finding the model helped convince Ross to become very aggressive in stopping and searching Iraqi "civilians." Iraqis heading south no longer had a free ticket to leave town. This proved to be a wise change. Over the next two days, Second Platoon and the rest of Golf Company would capture scores of Iraqi soldiers, irregulars, and Baath Party officials trying to leave An-Nasiriyah to the south.

Now that RCT-2 and 2/8 had the Iraqi resistance on the run, information about the whereabouts of Jessica Lynch started to build. On March 27, S. Sgt. Kevin Ellicott of Golf Company had received a handwritten letter, allegedly from Lynch, delivered by the now well-known Mohammed the lawyer. Mohammed would make a few more trips back to the Saddam Hospital in western An-Nasiriyah at the request of U.S. military intelligence. Later in the day on the 27th, as First Squad-Second Platoon was clearing one of the nicer homes in the city, David turned a corner into a side courtyard, his SAW in firing position, and found three Iraqi men standing in the yard.

In a split-second decision, he held his fire, judging they posed no threat. One man started talking to him in decent English. "No shoot, no shoot, friend, not enemy!" he told David. "There is American woman soldier in Saddam Hospital," he said. By now Sgt. Campbell and radioman Miguel had entered the courtyard. "Who are these two guys?" Campbell asked. "They bodyguards," the man replied. "Well they can leave; we'll talk to you," Campbell told the informant. "He told us the whole story of Jessica Lynch," David said. "He had a lot of details right that we already knew were fact, but the Saddam Hospital was news to us. He was also smoking a joint—probably nervous," David said later.

Campbell passed this corroborating information up the chain of command. Two days later, an Iraqi citizen walked up to Kerry Sanders and told him Lynch was still alive in the Saddam Hospital. Kerry in turn reported the information to TAC. "From March 25 to April 1, every day we received human intelligence on Jessica Lynch from people on the street," Fulford recalled, all of which was passed up the chain to RCT-2. "We knew she was in the Saddam Hospital; we didn't know what condition she was in. Reports varied widely from 'She's fine,' to 'She's dead,' to 'She's going to be executed,' to 'She's going to have her leg amputated.'"

The evidence of Jessica Lynch's location had by the 27th

become sufficiently strong enough for action to be taken. On March 28, U.S. Special Forces began final preparations for the rescue of Lynch. In addition to wounded American POWs, there were reports that the villainous "Chemical Ali"—the man who had used chemical weapons to kill thousands of Kurds in northern Iraq—was using the Saddam Hospital and surrounding areas as his headquarters. This meant there were significant numbers of Iraqi Army personnel in and around the hospital. And it meant they would have to be dealt with before a rescue could be attempted.

The Special Forces with Marine air and artillery support began conducting a systematic reduction of the Iraqi forces in the area of the Saddam Hospital. Also brought in were Air Force C130 Spectre gunships—large four-engine turboprop cargo planes converted to carry a number of large caliber automatic cannons. For three days the Iraqi positions were pounded. During the late night of April 1 and into the early morning of the April 2, Dunahoe's Third Battalion-Second Marines of RCT-2 and Second Battalion-First Marines—the ground unit from the Fifteenth MEU—engaged the remaining Iraqi forces in the vicinity of the hospital, while the Special Forces team slipped in and rescued Jessica Lynch. The news of the rescue traveled fast. "The word was going around right after it happened," David recalled. "We were pumped!"

Intelligence played a vital role throughout the war and in Lynch's rescue in particular, and Mortenson later gave a glowing review of the excellent intelligence work of Dupree.

"John Dupree was an amazing Marine officer. He had the capacity to give me something that I had only heard about as a Marine officer in my entire career," Mortenson later described. "The standard joke is, most battalion level intel officers 'give you the weather report.'... What I needed to know is, 'What do you think?' I needed some analysis here....I needed him to take in all the information he could—from his human exploitation teams, from the scout-sniper reports, from the company reports, from higher headquarters, from imagery, from his own experience, from the psychological operations team, from the civil affairs detachment that I had with me.

"He brought all that info together and was able to create his own S2 section. He synthesized it, and he was able to communicate that to Rob Fulford and me in such a manner that it actually impacted and helped decision-making. It helped shape decision-making. He was extraordinary at it."

Dupree and his team did a terrific job of providing this "ground truth" tactical human intel straight off the battlefield, which proved to be the best and most helpful intel Mortenson received of all the various sources. The importance of the roles fulfilled by the staff officers and the executive officer in a battalion may be under-emphasized and under-reported in general, but they are absolutely vital to the BC, and Mortenson had picked exceptional Marines for these positions. Throughout the conflict Mortenson relied heavily upon the advice of Fulford and Dupree in TAC and Alford in Main, and the input of these officers proved invaluable.

By this time in the battle for An-Nasiriyah, it had become clear to many of the men of 2/8 that their excellent results and miraculously few casualties were due to more than just their expert skills and execution. They had been protected by the very hand of God the whole time in combat. CAAT Platoon Commander MacCutcheon personified this fact. His platoon had fought the enemy in direct engagements for five straight days in An-Nasiriyah, against some formidable weapons systems including the ZSUs and D30 artillery. It is undeniably miraculous that none of his sixteen Humvees were disabled by enemy fire then and throughout the remainder of the war.

MacCutcheon told Chaplain Rogers after about a week of fighting, "You know Chaplain, I think your prayers are working! I haven't had a single vehicle destroyed, and not one has broken down during combat." Rogers later explained, "This is very unusual; you typically would at least see some tires blow out from being hit, but we didn't even have that happen!" Many other Marines acknowledged the Lord as well.

On March 30, David made a "field postcard" from the cardboard backing off an MRE package. He wrote home, "God's blessings to y'all. He's been taking care of me here.... We've been in some firefights, and a lot has been going on. The Lord has been protecting me. I am fine, and proud to be doing my job.... Love you all dearly. Dave."

Fulford would later summarize the miraculous results that 2/8 had experienced. "I truly believe we had an umbrella of protection. There is no question in my mind that the Lord's hand was in the overall protection of the battalion. A number of things happened; artillery rounds landing within our position and nobody being injured, our CAAT Platoon was engaged five straight days with some fairly heavy weapon systems from the enemy shooting at them, and not a single vehicle was destroyed from our side! Not one destroyed!" Also miraculous, he said, was the fact that no one was killed when Main Command Post was hit, and transitioned into a friendly fire incident.

The last few days of March and first two days of April saw 2/8 continuing mop-up combat operations. Back home in western New York, our family could sense as we prayed that the situation in An-Nasiriyah was now tilted heavily in favor of Task Force Tarawa. Late in the evening of March 29—early in the morning of the 30th in Iraq—our family was impressed by the Holy Spirit to pray that the Iraqi soldiers would be convinced that there is no honor in dying for a wicked man and that there is no dishonor in surrendering to a just cause. Evidently this manner of prayer helped, because the last few days in March saw both Golf and Echo Company capture scores of Iraqi soldiers, most of whom had lost any fighting spirit they may have had a week earlier.

On March 30, 2/8 found large caches of weapons in buildings in the south side of the city. On April 1, Golf Company cleared an aluminum and textile factory and found more weapons caches. Clearly, the battle for An-Nasiriyah was winding down. On April 3, the Twenty-Fourth MEU entered the city and relieved RCT-2 and 2/8. The battle for An-Nasiriyah had been won. Task Force Tarawa's new orders were to head north. The next assignment for Mortenson and 2/8: advance to the town of Ad-Diwaneyah.

9

MORE MISSIONS, MORE SUCCESS

For He has done marvelous things; His right hand and His holy arm have gained Him the victory.

—PSALM 98:1

Out of the mouth of babes and nursing infants You have ordained strength, because of Your enemies, that you may silence the enemy and the avenger.

—PSALM 8:2

Marines constantly seek to adapt new techniques, organization, and procedures to the realities of the environment. . . . The ability to adapt enables Marines to be comfortable within an environment dominated by friction.

—FROM *LEADING MARINES*

O N APRIL 4, THE DAY after they left An-Nasiriyah, 2/8 reached the town of Ad-Diwaneyah. There were no large concentrated Iraqi forces in the city, either regular Army or Fedayeen. But there was a major weapons depot found. In the United States early in the morning of Saturday, April 5, Kerry Sanders reported on NBC news that 2/8 had taken control of 120 buildings full of weapons and ammunition. It was a huge supply. "There was a lot of ammo there, designed to support division-sized regular Army units," Mortenson said. Dupree added, "It had Soviet-style bunkers, a typical, old Soviet ammo facility."

Golf Company was assigned to guard and inventory the facility. A little excitement came via the television news when a former

U.N. weapons inspector saw munitions from live TV footage that he didn't recognize and stated: "You may have something there." Golf Company then went in with protective suits and tested the unknown munitions for activations, which turned up negative. The unknown munitions and the accompanying instructions for use were of Russian origin. Dupree located two Marines of ethnic Polish heritage who could read Russian and had them translate the labeling. It turned out the munitions were short-range rockets used for launching line charges over minefields to detonate and clear them.

Ad-Diwaneyah was not calm at all, with an LAR unit from Task Force Tarawa involved in an engagement, and units from 2/8 on the outskirts of the city flushing out a few individual snipers and wiping out two small Iraqi ambushes. The orders for 2/8 kept them from entering, in part to allow other U.S. forces to work in the city. After four days in Ad-Diwaneyah, a small number of 2/8 forces remained on the perimeter to provide security operations and to support some Special Forces' operations in the vicinity. The bulk of 2/8 moved on to the town of Al-Shumali, about 40 miles from Ad-Diwaneyah.

Golf Company occupied the town proper and found Al-Shumali peaceful. They received a warm reception from the Iraqi citizens there. Even so, Ross took nothing for granted and the company conducted patrols and continued with typical combat operations, but found no organized Iraqi resistance. From April 13 to April 15, 2/8 moved to the town of Al-Aziziyah, located close to the intersection of the Tigris and Euphrates rivers, and remained alert in combat operation mode but again found no organized resistance.

The relative break in the action in Al-Aziziyah afforded Mortenson and Alford some time to banter over their respective command-post locations. "I was mad at Alford," Mortenson later recalled in jest. "He and Main had a better site than I did with TAC!" While Mortenson's TAC CP was a bullet-ridden, heavily damaged building, Alford and Main had managed to find a pristine abandoned Iraqi Army building. After Al-Aziziyah, the battalion moved back to Al-Shumali for three days, from April 16 until April 18.

One of the most incredible answers to prayer seen over the

month, from the start of the war on March 19 until April 18, was the supernatural stamina and endurance that many of the 2/8 Marines experienced. David experienced this in a big way and described it later in detail. "Over that month I averaged less than two hours of sleep per night. One day, March 27, we got eight hours of sleep; two other nights I got about five hours sleep; many nights I didn't sleep at all; and the rest of the nights I had one to two hours of sleep, max. The other guys were good to go, too!" These young men had experienced a miraculous, direct answer to the "Elijah prayer" of many believers back home. "It was almost weird," David said later. "I always had energy, and I knew it was the Lord. I was always volunteering for patrols and guard duty. Just like Elijah in 1 Kings, the Spirit of the Lord came upon me. I got so used to it, I didn't think about it."

A quick calculation from David's testimony reveals he managed around forty-five hours of sleep over thirty-one days, or approximately 90 minutes a night. And despite the twenty-two or more hours of activity each day, David lost only five pounds. There is no natural explanation for this when fully functioning in combat operations for such an extended period with little sleep. Surely the Lord answered the prayers of His people!

Everywhere 2/8 went in Iraq, they found ample evidence of organized, institutional hatred and malice on the part of Hussein's Baath regime toward Americans and Jews, and Christians in particular. Virtually every primary and secondary school David's Second Platoon entered had artwork on display glorifying the terrorist attacks of September 11. From An-Nasiriyah through the town of Ad-Diwaneyah and later into Al-Kut, 2/8 overran several training camps used by the Iraqi Army and by terrorists. Typically, the pistol and rifle ranges in these sites had caricatures of Jews and Christians as targets.

Dupree later explained Saddam Hussein's actions and goals in detail. "[Hussein] supported terrorism, and terrorism against Israel. In fact, Hussein's Fedayeen's original mission was to be an army to help liberate Palestine.... There were a few things he publicly stated that he wanted to do as president. He wanted to unite the Arab nations, he wanted to be Nebuchadnezzar, he wanted to destroy the Jews and get them out of Palestine, and he wanted to rule Iraq. In all these training camps we went into, he had made caricatures of Jews, and hung them up on pistol targets. One caricature had a Jew with a Star of David tattoo on his forehead, with a yarmulke on his head; and the image had fangs and was demonized. He was actively supporting the destruction of Jews. He actively supported terrorism."

Though the sponsoring of terrorism against Israel, the United States, and Western culture and the several direct attacks launched on Israel by Saddam Hussein over the last 30 years seem to be easily forgotten in America, it is a safe bet that none of these young Marines who fought so hard to topple Hussein will ever forget what they saw in Iraq. They know firsthand that he was a very real enemy to their country.

The relative calm and break in intensity of operations from April 3 to April 18 gave the men of 2/8 time to write letters and the opportunity to receive letters and packages from home. On April 5 Fulford called home from Ad-Diwaneyah using Kerry Sanders' cell phone. Fulford had received on March 31, while still in An-Nasiriyah, what he later called a "bizarre" order from Maj. Gen. James Mattis, CO of the First Marine Division, to call his father. Mattis had been a BC under Fulford's father during the Persian Gulf War, and he apparently was trying to do the Fulford family a favor. Unable to find time for several days to make the call, Fulford finally placed the call on Sunday the 5th.

Fulford spoke to his mother, who told him he would be amazed at the number of people around the world who were praying for him by name. His parents had been receiving letters from people in Hawaii, where he attended high school, from several more states in the United States, and from people in Germany where his parents had been stationed when his father retired from the Marines. After the war, when discussing the difference prayer support had made in the success of 2/8, Fulford recalled, "That was the moment I knew; it hadn't registered with me the magnitude of it prior to that call."

Those times in early to mid-April for reflection about the favor and goodness of God weren't limited to just 2/8 Marines within

RCT-2. Many Marines of Brent Dunahoe's 3/2 had become believers over the previous few months—some undoubtedly because they also had experienced the miraculous protection of Almighty God. On Easter Sunday, April 20, Chaplain Brian White of 3/2 baptized about thirty new believers in the waters of the Tigris River. In addition, a sergeant from RCT-2 who had been a practicing Muslim, converted to Christianity during Operation Iraqi Freedom, and he too was water baptized in the Easter Sunday service. Later, Regimental Chaplain Ritchie, somewhat still amazed, recalled, "On Easter Sunday morning we baptized a Muslim into the Christian faith in a Muslim country!"

Events again began to heat up for 2/8 in mid-April. On Good Friday, April 18, 2/8 was ordered to the city of Al-Kut, close to the Iranian border. The orders that day from Brig. Gen.Natonski in Task Force Tarawa split Col. Bailey's RCT-2 into two units. Bailey, his staff headquarters and 1/2, 1/10, and the attached LAR, Engineer, and Recon Companies were ordered to move back south and conduct a relief in place of the 11th MEU. Both 2/8 and 3/2 were then placed under the direct command of Brig. Gen. Natonski, with 3/2 sent to An-Numuniyah and 2/8 ordered to Al-Kut. The move to occupy Al-Kut quickly brought the Marines of 2/8 into sharp focus again.

No U.S. forces had actually entered the city before 2/8. A city of 300,000 residents, Al-Kut was also headquarters to the Baghdad Division of the Republican Guard. The I MEF had destroyed the Baghdad Division in their drive to the Iraqi capital, but there were still some elements of the decimated division in and around the city when 2/8 arrived. Fulford later explained the military situation in layman's terms, "There were some folks hanging around who still wanted to fight." Politically, the matter was complicated by various elements all vying for control of the city. Followers of the Muslim extremist al-Sadr, of the Iranian-backed BADR Corps, and of the moderate Grand Ayatollah Sistani all were competing to fill the power vacuum. An influential thug of unknown association named "Abbas" had barricaded himself and followers in a key government building. Added to these problems was much civil unrest including riots, extensive looting, and sniper fire from various factions of thugs.

Mortenson later described the chaotic situation in detail. "There was no law enforcement. The city was being run by thugs. The 10 percent of the population that were acting as criminals were intimidating the remaining 90 percent of the population that just wanted to live their lives. I equate it to what would happen in your hometown if tomorrow there was no fire department, there was no police department, there were no hospitals and all the doctors were gone, every piece of civil control was gone, garbage collection didn't exist. If all that infrastructure that supports your city where you live, when you woke up tomorrow, was gone, I would argue that your life would be ruled by the 5 percent or 10 percent of your community that is evil. These 10 percent have no problem intimidating with violence and engaging in violence on those that would not. I would argue it would happen in any city in the world." Fulford later summarized the situation succinctly, stating, "Al-Kut was considered a powder keg waiting to explode."

Furthermore, with the fall of Baghdad a few days earlier, formal heavy fighting was subsiding. While remaining in combat operations, 2/8 would now have to transition toward stability and support operations. "It was a difficult environment," Mortenson later stated. "The Marines were now being asked to be even more discerning in their use of force. I was asking them to be a little bit more discretionary."

Natonski had ordered Mortenson to stabilize the city for very important reasons. First, 2/8 needed to provide security to enable Natonski and his staff to establish relationships with Grand Ayatollah Sistani and his followers. Second, Natonski needed 2/8 to deal with the criminal elements and create a secure environment to enable Task Force Tarawa's civil affairs group to begin the process of rebuilding the infrastructure of the city. Natonski had personally pulled Mortenson aside to explain his objectives for the city and review the situation. Mortenson later recalled, "The city was ready for it. General Natonski's intuition was correct."

Mortenson and his staff quickly came up with a plan of action and began to execute immediately. Deciding in his words to "manage the city in chunks," Mortenson assigned each of his Rifle companies management of a sector of the city. To ensure that he would be able to react quickly to any situation with plenty of force, Mortenson created a mobile-reserve element under Alford's command and affectionately named it "Task Force Rebel," after Alford's call sign. Task Force Rebel consisted of Lieutenant Fitzsimmons' Second Platoon from Golf Company, an LAR Platoon with seven LAVs, a CAAT section with four Humvees, and a unit of combat engineers. To be effective as a reserve unit meant that Task Force Rebel would need to be able to respond quickly to any trouble that arose. Mortenson decided to station the task force in the northern part of Al-Kut in a confluence of roads that would allow Alford and his Marines to move rapidly into any of the sectors of the city to reinforce Echo, Fox, or Golf Companies.

The plan called for 2/8 to move in quickly and occupy the city all at once. "We didn't do it from outside in," Mortenson explained later. "The battalion went in and sat down in their neighborhoods, occupied buildings, and began patrolling the streets literally overnight." Under the cover of darkness on the night of April 18, Mortenson moved 2/8 into the city. On the morning of April 19 the people of Al-Kut awoke to see Marines on patrol in every sector of the city. Mortenson recalled, "The townspeople went to bed on the night of the 18th, and when they woke up on the morning of the 19th there were Marine squads walking down the streets providing security for that city. It was a stark awakening for the bad guys still in town." Suddenly, to quote one of Mortenson's favorite phrases, "There was a new sheriff in town."

The battalion, in conjunction with Special Forces, quickly crushed the lingering military threats from the Baghdad Division. "We had a few skirmishes, with a few Iraqis killed, with no Marine injuries," Fulford said later. Luciano had to authorize only two fire-support missions, one an artillery barrage in support of the Special Forces, and the other an attack helicopter mission that destroyed an Iraqi mortar site. Mortenson recalled, "We had some events and we killed some people that needed killing. But nowhere near the volume of the combat level of ops that we had in An-Nasiriyah." Almost all of 2/8's efforts went into the work of civilian and political control.

The first troublemakers Alford went after were the looters, and he used Fitzsimmons' Second Platoon as his "muscle." Much of the looting going on throughout the country after Baghdad fell in mid-April was being carried out by hardened criminals who had been released from jail by Hussein just before the war started. Of an estimated 100,000 prisoners released by Hussein, the consensus opinion of experts was that 75,000 were true criminals and the rest were political prisoners. Many of the 75,000 went back to their hometowns where they terrorized the general civilian population. Brazenly looting in broad daylight, they would drive up to stores and businesses, park their vehicles in front of their intended targets, and proceed to loot. With a non-existent police force, these criminals were having a field day in Al-Kut until Alford and Fitzsimmons arrived with Second Platoon.

On April 19, the Second Platoon's first day in Al-Kut, Alford set up "nonlethal ambushes." Dividing his men into teams, he placed them inside likely targets. As the looters would enter stores and buildings, two or three Marines would collar them, handcuff them, and collect them in a pile. At the end of the first day, David's team had captured fifteen looters. Alford handed his first day's haul over to the Free Iraqi Forces (FIF), assuming they would hold the thieves for civilian trial at some point down the road. For reasons unknown, the FIF released the prisoners the very next day—and true to their nature the thieves went right back to stealing.

Called in again to quell looting on April 21, Second Platoon Marines recognized the same vehicles being used from two days earlier. Alford and Fitzsimmons had had it with these criminals and moved to more forceful measures. Seizing the vehicles, they then unleashed Second Platoon to round up and chase the thieves down. Keeping the looters as their own prisoners this time, the word spread fast that these Marines meant business. Responsible Iraqi citizens started cooperating with Second Platoon and were sincerely thanking them for rounding up the thugs. "He ali-baba"—Arabic for "thief"—they would tell the platoon Marines, pointing at thugs trying to blend in with normal citizens. The vast majority of the looting stopped almost immediately after April 21.

The first several days in Al-Kut also saw riots. Mortenson explained later, "The riffraff in Al-Kut had released criminals, Iraqi Army guys who are back in their civilian attire, and unemployment in Al-Kut at this time is probably 100 percent.... They're breaking into each other's shops, they're doing violence on government buildings because they're angry at Saddam Hussein, they're ransacking their own libraries and their own schools because they're angry." Mortenson quickly had the Rifle Company and Task Force Rebel Marines trained in riot control techniques.

Using an active crowd-control strategy, Second Platoon would line up with face and large body shields near an unruly mob, centering their shield line on the two or three agitators in the crowd. Upon command, the Marine line would push open a hole in the crowd, something akin to offensive linemen in football creating a hole for the running back to shoot through. Other Marines called snatchers would rush through the hole, grab the agitators, and pull them back behind the shield line which would then quickly close the hole. The agitators would be handcuffed, arrested and brought back to the Marine compound as prisoners. Once the agitators were carted off, the crowds usually dispersed fairly quickly.

To further quell civilian unrest and to reinforce the unequivocal message that they meant business, 2/8 continually ran patrols, secured schools and government buildings, performed house-to-house searches, and cordoned off key streets, not allowing anyone or any vehicle passage. Arabic translators would stand with Marine guards at the ends of the cordoned areas, warning people approaching that they would be shot if they attempted to pass the Marines. And with the word out that Marine sniper teams were looking for a good reason to shoot, the factional sniping ended quickly. "In six days we had Al-Kut locked down and peaceful," David said later.

The battalion also made short work of Abbas' stronghold as well. It was situated in Yeo's Echo Company sector, and from the time Echo had started patrols on April 19 Abbas had been having his followers come out of the building to demonstrate against the Marines' presence. Yeo got tired of that nonsense very quickly, so he decided to make life miserable for Abbas and his thugs. Yeo made sure that a patrol from Echo went by Abbas' location just about every hour, around the clock, every day. Abbas' men thus got no sleep with the constant presence of Echo Marines. After a couple of days of this Abbas' men got tired and erected a barricade to attempt to block the path of Marine patrols. With this feeble attempt Abbas was now interfering with the mission of Echo Company, so Mortenson and Yeo decided it was time to take Abbas down.

They coordinated a simultaneous assault on Abbas' municipal building compound using two Rifle Platoons, one each from Echo and Golf, and a CAAT Section. The CAAT Humvees burst through the front gate of the compound at the same time the Rifle platoons breeched the municipal building walls. With close to 100 Marines in bad moods quickly upon them, Abbas' followers were overwhelmed. "We wrestled control from that guy over the first week or so," Ross recalled. "We took the municipal building down that the Abbas guy was using as his headquarters, and we found some weapons. The guy had already left, but we did capture some of his lieutenants."

While 2/8 provided security, the civil affairs section of Task Force Tarawa began to rebuild the city infrastructure. "USMC civil affairs personnel used that municipal building to set up a provisional government for the city and province," Ross explained. "Marines did a great job of cleaning up the place. Then we invited local civilians; school superintendents; power, water, fire department people and others, who came in to meet with Marine civilian affairs personnel.... The Iraqi civil leaders were a bit overwhelmed—they were inquisitive about American government functions. They were used to top-down dealings, and simple questions like the amount of school supplies needed they couldn't answer at first. They asked for time to go ask the teachers."

There were a variety of dangerous situations for 2/8 Marines during their time in Al-Kut, and God continued to protect 2/8 by providing insight and opportune words of wisdom, at times from unlikely sources. Yeo experienced one such godsend in an amazing way. Throughout the first ten days in the city, Yeo regularly saw a young girl, around seven years of age, following Echo Company patrols. The father of three daughters himself, Yeo naturally took notice of the young girl. But what he found quite curious was she was seemingly everywhere his patrols went. Most kids had a fairly small, well-defined area that their parents allowed them to roam and play in, but this little girl apparently had free reign within Echo's whole sector. Her clothes and skin were always clean, so she wasn't an abandoned street child. She also spoke a few words in English, and learned words fast as Yeo began to interact with her. He would sneak her candy and care packages, making sure the older children didn't steal them from her. Yeo eventually met her family, who owned a small store, and he made sure they received a good share of aid and gifts.

Around April 28 Yeo was on patrol at about 3 p.m. with Echo Company's Third Platoon. They were near the girl's family's store when a couple of spiteful-looking sixteen- to seventeen-year-old teenagers approached the platoon. "We know where there are lots of weapons—we'll take you there," they told Yeo's Marines. The little girl immediately got Yeo's attention, walked over to him and held his hand, and then pointed at the teenagers and said, "bad." Yeo picked up on her warning and began to get cautious thoughts as well. *These guys have no good will toward us; it's a set-up*, he thought, and sent them on their way, telling them the platoon was busy but would come by later. Getting his interpreter, Yeo began to question the young girl. It turned out the teenagers were associated with Abbas, the ringleader whose municipal building headquarters had been overrun by Yeo's Marines.

Yeo turned the tables on the set-up. Waiting until 1 a.m., he sent Third Platoon to investigate and clear the building identified by the teenagers. There they surprised about eight Iraqi men and confiscated some weapons and ammunition. Yeo later stated, "We don't know how many guys were there waiting for us that afternoon."

Reflecting on this incredible word of protection provided through the seven-year-old girl, Yeo's wife, Andrea; mother, Delores; and sister-in-law Patricia Williams reached the same conclusion. They believe this was God's way of protecting Yeo and Echo

Company from harm. God had provided an answer to their family's and friends' prayers this time in a most unexpected manner.

For Fox Company, Al-Kut was fairly uneventful. The company used a university as its base of operations, and the college administrators were happy to see the Marines there because of the looting that had been ongoing. First Lt. Chad Ragan had been moved over to become Fox Company XO, and he recalled that other than being shot at a few times—usually poorly aimed pot-shots taken at night—there wasn't much action for Fox. Cpl. Friend was leading a patrol that ended up engaging in a running gun battle with a couple of thugs of unknown association who finally fled in a small van. Fox Marines also made some weapons seizures and broke up a couple of meetings of young Iraqi men who seemed to be up to no good, but otherwise saw little action.

Throughout their time in Iraq, the men of 2/8 had views of the civilian population that ran the gamut from extreme poverty to opulence. Al-Kut provided some of the most difficult images for the Marines. Dupree earnestly recalled the sights. "The most troubling aspect of Al-Kut was a group living in abject poverty on one side of a street, with others living in palaces on the other side. You had camel-dung construction on one side and palaces on the other—mostly Baath Party officials. You saw undernourished kids on one side and overweight kids of Baath Party officials across from them." There were other hard-to-take scenes as well. It was common to drive by a farm and see the father and sons sitting on the front porch drinking tea while the mother and daughters were tending the fields. David would later say that such ungracious and inconsiderate behavior on the part of Iraqi men really annoyed him and his buddies.

There were, however, some light-hearted moments in Al-Kut. When first entering the city, Golf Company had come upon a young women's private high school. Given the general state of lawlessness at the time, Iraqi teenage boys had been regularly jumping the fence into the school compound and committing acts of theft and vandalism. Seeing the Marines approaching, the headmistress of the school, who spoke English fluently, came out to Capt. Ross. "Please help us," she pleaded, explaining the situation. Ross replied,

"I've got just the Marine to help you, ma'am." Calling for Torres of Second Platoon, the skilled boxer, Ross told him to see to it that no one got by. Sure enough, just a little while later a couple of teenage boys tried scaling the fence, only to be greeted rather abruptly by Torres. The boy problems at the school ended that day.

The battalion remained in Al-Kut for twenty-four days, until May 11, gradually being relieved in a four-day turnover starting May 7. Third Battalion-Twenty-Third Marines, a Marine reserve unit from Louisiana and an MP company from the Army's Eighty-Second Airborne Division were their relief. Mortenson had received orders for 2/8 to re-embark on the USS Saipan and USS Kearsarge in Kuwait for the return trip home. From the evening firefight of March 26 until May 11, a period of 46 days, 2/8 did not sustain a single casualty from the enemy, or by accident or from an unruly civilian crowd. The mission for 2/8 in Iraq had come to its end. It was time to go home.

Every Marine in 2/8 who had left Camp Lejeune back in January to face an uncertain future would be coming home. Not one Marine had lost an arm, leg, eye, finger, or toe while in Iraq. Chaplain Rogers' prayers on the first day of the war had been answered. Amazingly, not one Marine from 2/8 had been wounded while riding in a battalion vehicle. As for vehicles, except for the trio of seven-ton trucks accidentally shot up by friendly fire and a couple of damaged Humvees left behind, every 2/8 vehicle would be returning home in working order, most of them unscathed. It had been an amazing, miracle-filled journey for all the Marines of 2/8.

Their efforts and superb results throughout the war did not go unnoticed. Later in 2003, President Bush honored all the Marines of I MEF including Task Force Tarawa and 2/8 by awarding them the Presidential Unit Citation (PUC), the highest combat decoration for unit performance in war. The units of I MEF, more than 60,000 men and women, thereby became the first Marines since Hue City in 1968 during the Vietnam War to receive the PUC. President Bush also awarded the PUC to the Army's Third Infantry Division.

Winning the PUC is an honor that for many servicemen is

more meaningful than individual awards, for it literally conveys the stamp of approval of the commander in chief for combat performance. It recognizes the excellence of the whole unit in combat, the effectiveness and results of the whole team. As for individual awards, as of May 2004 numerous combat decorations had been awarded to 2/8 Marines, including thirteen Bronze Stars with more still being processed. Mortenson's ultimate team concept that had been forged from eighteen months of rigorous training proved successful in combat and resulted in 2/8 earning the highest honors. The Marines of 2/8 had, simply put, performed brilliantly.

10

THE RIDE HOME

We went through fire and through water; but You brought us out
to rich fulfillment. ... But certainly God has heard me; He has
attended to the voice of my prayer. Blessed be God, who has not
turned away my prayer, nor His mercy from me!

—PSALM 66:12, 19-20

The bond which grows among warriors who, together, experience
great danger in the crucible of war is difficult to describe.

—FROM *LEADING MARINES*

THE MEN OF 2/8 RETURNED to Kuwait by air transport
and by truck convoy over the two days of May 10 and
11. One of the first things most of them did was take a
shower. "I had my first shower in two months on May 11 back in
Kuwait," David recalled. "I took three showers that day!" With
Echo Company embarking on the *Kearsarge* and the balance of
2/8 along with units of MAG 29 loading on the *Saipan*, 2/8 set
sail on May 13 for the ride home.

David managed to call home from the *Saipan* on the 14th,
just two days after his twentieth birthday. His voice was sky high.
We could feel his joy and excitement over the phone. "I was so
happy," he would recall. "I had Holy Spirit joy!"

154

The officers all agreed that the several week transit time to come home was a very good thing. "The ship ride home was a benefit," Mortenson said. Ross explained: "The ride, five weeks, was a good time to decompress, to work through issues." Fulford concurred: "Coming back home on ship was very productive. Chaplain Rogers and the other chaplains had a very dynamic de-briefing program." Rogers and Chaplain Poole of MAG 29 developed and ran what they called the "Warrior Transition Program." It afforded the Marines the opportunity to discuss openly in groups or privately in one-on-one sessions what was most helpful to them during the war and to talk about events they had experienced.

The large size of the *Kearsarge* and *Saipan* allowed the Marines the option of participating in a wide variety of activities. Many took advantage of those options. Chaplain Rogers started up Bible studies again, which David, Rodriguez and others participated in. "The Marines who went to the Bible studies and church services on the way over also participated on the way back, but a lot of guys now had different perspectives," David said. "There was much thankfulness among the men, a deeper understanding of the graciousness of God."

David slept a lot, worked out in the gym nearly every day, attended church services and Chaplain Rogers' Bible studies, prayed and read a couple of Christian books provided by Erin Hawkins and Rodriguez. Ryans participated in Bible studies and sang in the ship's choir. "That really helped me decompress," he said later. He also enjoyed spending time with his fellow company commanders talking about events.

Capt. Yeo experienced a huge sense of relief on the *Kearsarge*. For him it was a time of thankfulness, of reflecting and thinking about lessons learned. He had good reason to be especially thankful. His Echo Company had zero casualties the whole time in Iraq—not even one casualty through all the heavy fighting in An-Nasiriyah. It really hit him clearly onboard as he received loads of mail from back home. His mother, Delores, had sent prayer tracts; his wife, Andrea, and mother and their prayer groups had sent letters; his sister-in-law and her friends from various high schools in South Dakota had sent letters with prayers. Yeo readily credited God for His protection. "There was divine intervention," he said. Yeo summarized the key factors in 2/8's success as "training, confidence, and belief in a just cause, and our beliefs."

Capt. Hackney, the *Saipan* CO, arranged a Memorial Day remembrance service on May 26. It was held in the huge hanger deck of the ship, and Mortenson was given the honor of addressing the sailors and Marines on board. He spoke with characteristically direct words. "For all of us remembrance has a deeper meaning now," he said. "The events and experiences of the last five months have cemented memories in the minds of each of us.... You have forged the bond of the 'Band of Brothers,' only attainable through war. Whether on the ground in places like An-Nasiriyah, A-Shumali or Salamon Pak; in the skies over Iraq; or the ever present afloat off the coast, all have endured and become a band of brothers—sailor and Marine.... You each have had a defining moment in this war.... And, as such, a common bond exists between each of you, a common bond that will be eternal, as eternal as the bond between God and our fallen comrades. However, we have been given the gift of life. So be ever thankful for this gift."

While the bulk of the battalion was steaming back to North Carolina, some of the Marines from 2/8 who had been sent home to recuperate from combat wounds experienced unexpected and exciting surprises. Lcpl. Josh Menard was invited to a reception where he met President George H. W. Bush, the 41st president of the United States. The senior President Bush was so impressed with Josh that on May 31 he e-mailed Capt. Dremann on the *Saipan* with the following gracious and heartfelt message:

Dear Capt. Dremann,

You may be surprised to receive this e-mail from a former Commander in Chief. I had the pleasure of helping welcome home Lcpl. Josh Menard, one of your proud Marines. Josh told me about Fox Company and his pride in his outfit.

I just wanted you and your Marines to know how proud I am of the job the Marines did in Iraq—Fox Company included. I wish for all of you a very safe return home. You will find that a grateful America awaits you, sharing the same pride I do in those who served.

When it comes to the Marine Corps and your service to our great country, I know that our president feels exactly the same way his Dad does. Bless 'em all! Semper Fi.

George Bush, 41ˢᵗ President

Dremann read the message to Fox Company. They were already sky-high from their incredible experience in Iraq, and this letter probably kicked them up a notch or two.

The *Saipan* made an R&R port call in Rota, Spain, in early June. The men of 2/8 took full advantage of the stay. Able to enjoy the town and nearby beaches in civilian attire, it was their first time of liberty in more than six months. The *Saipan's* Morale, Welfare and Recreation officer had prearranged some twenty excursions to various locations in Spain, many of them two to three days long, for the Marines to select from. Winery tours, trips to Madrid and Mediterranean beaches, deep-sea fishing excursions, and shopping trips all were available and sold out fast.

But Mortenson wasn't about to let the port call detract much from his goal of getting all his men back to Camp Lejeune and their families. The last thing he needed was to have 700 Marines still coming off combat intensity running amok through Rota for a few days and nights. He allowed those 2/8 Marines not participating in the formal excursions to enjoy the days but ordered them to return to the *Saipan* and sleep on the ship each night. Mortenson established late curfews by rank and responsibilities—the more senior in rank, the later the curfew. The officers and senior NCOs would be the last to return to ship and would effectively sweep the commercial establishments in Rota to ensure the lower ranks had safely returned to ship. And fortunately no Marine behaved badly enough to earn a one-on-one meeting with 1st Sgt. Squires. Squires didn't have his Chesty Puller portrait, anyway.

Unfortunately for Yeo and Echo Company on the *Kearsarge*, their ship was diverted to Liberia on the ride home to provide support for Americans, if needed, in that politically unstable country. Fortunately they did not have to deploy to shore, and Echo returned to North Carolina six days later than the rest of 2/8 on the *Saipan*.

On June 22, the *Saipan* moored off Morehead City, North

Carolina, to disembark. The Marines loaded into their landing craft to ferry from the *Saipan* to shore. While in transit over the water, their first "official" greeting was an attractive young woman in a bikini standing in a small boat and holding a "Welcome Home Marines" sign. "Everybody started yelling," David said. The Marines of 2/8 were definitely back in America.

The Marines had hired buses to transport the battalion for the short forty-five minute drive from Morehead City to Camp Lejeune. All along the ride they were welcomed by huge homemade signs hanging from bridges, signs posted on the sides of the highways, and by scores of cars and trucks blaring horns as they drove by. In addition to 2/8, most of the other units within RCT-2 and Task Force Tarawa arrived back in Camp Lejeune the same day. Thousands of Marines, friends, and family members were being reunited.

At Lejeune, the rear party of 2/8 led by Gunny Sergeant Minton had organized a large welcome home party at the battalion's building complex. Friends and families streamed in, and Kerry Sanders showed up with his crew and televised the event live on NBC. It was an emotional, joyful event attended by a few thousand people. Our family arrived at 10:30 a.m. for the scheduled noontime arrival of the battalion, and the battalion complex was already teeming with people. For the wives, mothers, fathers, and families of the 2/8 Marines, this was an unforgettable day. Catherine Dremann beautifully reflected the sentiment of the wives when she later recalled, "There was an unexplainable joy. Nothing at that moment was wrong." A few days later she poignantly described the event in her journal:

> I can't begin to explain the emotion. It was better than my wedding day. I knew what was coming home. I wasn't starting a life with this wonderful man; through the grace of God I was being allowed to continue it.

For the Marines of 2/8, this was a sweet end to an unforgettable experience. They had prepared for, fought in, survived, and even prospered in war, and they all were now home. Surely, God saw them through.

EPILOGUE

"THE LORD ALONE KNOWS THE length of our days." As Major Rob Fulford and I sat to review a draft of this manuscript, he made this statement and encouraged me to remind readers of this fact. His point is very well-taken. During Operation Iraqi Freedom, Rob and his Second Battalion-Eighth Marines experienced numerous miracles of protection possible only by the hand of God Almighty. This book has in large part been an attempt to document some of what he and his fellow Marines experienced. And yet, just two or three miles to his north, another highly capable battalion from the same Regiment, First Battalion-Second Marines, experienced eighteen killed in action on the very first day of engagements, within the first few hours of the battle. God alone knows our days.

There are certain questions that we simply cannot answer. We know that Lt. Col. Mortenson and his staff of officers and senior noncommissioned officers did a superb job of training and leading 2/8. We also know that God moved His people to pray for individual Marines in 2/8 and for the battalion as a whole. We have read examples of how God answered those prayers by providing miraculous protection at times when 2/8 Marines were vulnerable and unable to protect themselves. But we can also be sure that every Marine battalion that fought in Operation Iraqi Freedom and lost Marines killed in action was expertly trained and led. We can be sure that some number of believers were praying for their protection as well. Why certain warriors die and others live is a mystery known only to God.

Jesus was confronted with a similar question one day during His ministry. A certain tower in the town of Siloam in Israel had fallen and killed eighteen people. Jesus told those listening that the eighteen who died were not worse people than the rest of them, that they were not more cursed than those still living. Rather, the real issue according to Jesus, was the need for all to repent and come to true faith in God. For, those without true faith will likewise perish.

This is our heartfelt cry for all who read this book. We believe this is the most important reason we were compelled to write the book in the first place. Listening to our oldest son, David, recount his own miraculous encounters with God, and seeing his faith built up and purified as a result—and then hearing more than a dozen other 2/8 Marines give similar testimony—gave us hope that many others could similarly have their faith strengthened. The degree to which this happens will be the only lasting measure of the success of this effort. May God bless you and may your trust and faith in our Lord and Savior Jesus Christ be built up as you read and reflect on this incredible true-life adventure.

Appendix I

Key to USMC and Related Abbreviations and Terms

BAS: battalion aid station

BC: battalion commander

CAS: close air support

CAAT: combined anti-armor anti-tank

CAX: combined arms exercise, realistic live fire training

CNN: the national cable news network

CO: commanding officer

CP: command post

CSSE: combat service support element

DOD: Department of Defense

EPW: enemy prisoner of war

G3: operations staff officer to a large unit led by a General officer

GPS: global positioning system—a satellite-based navigation system

H&S: headquarters and service company

HET: human exploitation team—an intelligence group

LAR: light armored reconnaissance

LAV: light armored vehicle

MAGTF: Marine Air-Ground Task Force

MAIN: the main command post—location of the XO and staff

MCT: Marine Combat Training

MEB: Marine Expeditionary Brigade, usually 12,000 to 15,000 Marines

MEF: Marine Expeditionary Force, usually 45,000 to 75,000 Marines

MEU: Marine Expeditionary Unit, usually 2,000 to 3,000 Marines

MK-19: Mark-19, a machine gun that fires 40 mm grenades

MLRS : Multiple Launch Rocket System, a powerful tactical rocket system

NEO: noncombatant evacuation operation

NCO: noncommissioned officer—i.e., sergeants and corporals

NBC: nuclear-biological-chemical

NBC-TV: the national news network

ORE: operational readiness evaluation

PT: physical training

RCT: Regimental Combat Team, a ground force of 4,000 to 6,000 Marines

RPG: rocket propelled grenade—Russian-designed weapon used by Iraqis

S2: intelligence officer in a battalion or regiment

S3: operations officer in a battalion or regiment

SAW: squad automatic weapon—a light machine gun

SOI: School of Infantry

TAA: tactical assembly area

TAC CP/TAC: tactical command post, headquarters to the battalion commander

TTP: tactics, techniques, and procedures

XO: executive officer, the person second in command in a unit

Appendix II

ORGANIZATIONAL CHART OF COALITION FORCES

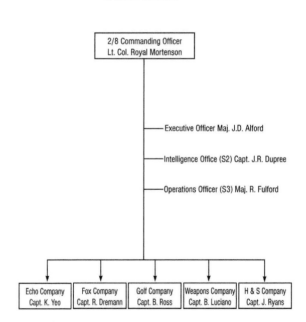

ORGANIZATIONAL CHART

2nd Battalion/8th Marines
Operation Iraqi Freedom

2/8 Commanding Officer
Lt. Col. Royal Mortenson

Executive Officer Maj. J.D. Alford

Intelligence Office (S2) Capt. J.R. Dupree

Operations Officer (S3) Maj. R. Fulford

| Echo Company Capt. K. Yeo | Fox Company Capt. R. Dremann | Golf Company Capt. B. Ross | Weapons Company Capt. B. Luciano | H & S Company Capt. J. Ryans |

ORGANIZATIONAL CHART

Coalition Forces
Start of Operation Iraqi Freedom

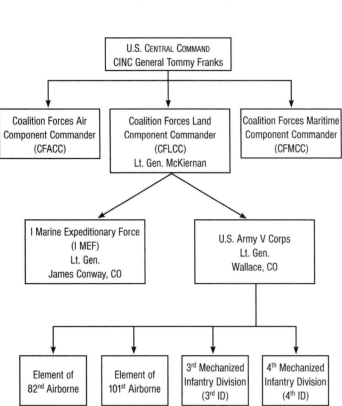

Appendix II: Oraganizational Chart of Coalition Forces

ORGANIZATIONAL CHART

I MEF–Operation Iraqi Freedom

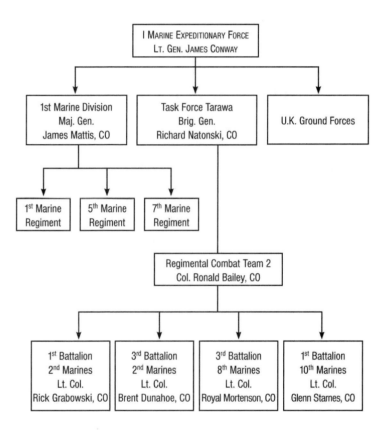

To Contact the Author

Glenn Alan Thomas
P.O. Box 100
East Amherst, NY 14051
gathomas57@yahoo.com